TALES
FROM
THE TOP

TALES
FROM
THE TOP

10 Vital Questions
Every Leader Must Answer to Stay
on Top of the Game

GRAHAM ALEXANDER

PIATKUS

Visit the Piatkus website!

Piatkus publishes a wide range of bestselling fiction and non-fiction, including books on health, mind, body & spirit, sex, self-help, cookery, biography and the paranormal.

If you want to:
- read descriptions of our popular titles
- buy our books over the internet
- take advantage of our special offers
- enter our monthly competition
- learn more about your favourite Piatkus authors

VISIT OUR WEBSITE AT: www.piatkus.co.uk

Copyright © 2005 Graham Alexander

Piatkus Books Ltd
5 Windmill Street
London W1T 2JA

email: info@piatkus.co.uk

The moral right of the author has been asserted

A catalogue record for this book is available from the British Library

ISBN 0 7499 2625 2

Edited by Andrew John
Text design by Paul Saunders

This book has been printed on paper manufactured
with respect for the environment using wood from
managed sustainable resources

Typesetting by Phoenix Photosetting, Chatham, Kent
Printed and bound in Great Britain by Biddles Ltd, King's Lynn, Norfolk

For Anita, Reina, Elan, Lara and Gucci –
the meaning in my life.

'Every leader knows it's lonely at the top. *Tales from the Top* takes this notion to a whole new dimension, providing today's business leaders with a way to think more clearly about how to lead better, live better, and feel better. Graham Alexander has produced a holy grail for leadership effectiveness.'

Michael Feiner, author of *The Feiner Points of Leadership*

'Graham's experienced, original, honest approach in helping business unit leaders improve themselves, which in turn improves the companies they run, is powerful and full of real work and world wisdom. *Tales from the Top* is a must read for managers and business leaders.'

Sam Bracken, Senior Consultant, FranklinCovey

Contents

Appendices

Acknowledgements

To my wife, Anita: This book and other commitments have meant sacrifices for which I give you profound thanks and my continuing love and support. You have always given the latter to me in abundance. And to the other loves of my life – my three children, Reina, Elan and Lara, who are the best and of whom I am enormously proud.

Thank you Echo Montgomery Garrett: You have worked tirelessly (including 4 am starts) to bring this book into reality. You have increasingly acted as my coach by suggesting ways to enhance the material, promote the book, raise my profile and so on. I thank you profoundly.

Thank you, Susan-Lucia Annunzio at the Centre for High Performance in Chicago for introducing me to my agent, Denise Marcil, and for being so supportive over so many years. Thank you, Denise, for suggesting Echo, and for securing me two terrific publishers. Thank you to Jonathan Merkh at Nelson Books and Judy Piatkus at Piatkus Books for your initial faith that I could produce this book and for being such delightful and easy partners throughout.

Thank you to all the leaders with whom I have worked and who have made this book possible. You work incredibly hard to do the best you can, and living life at the optimum isn't easy. Having led a business myself, I have enormous respect for your efforts and for the difficulty of the undertaking. From one warrior to another – keep on keeping on.

Finally, thank you, Mother and Father. My mother is most impressed that I have produced books. My father – sadly no longer with us – would, I believe, have been fascinated by this book and would have pored over it for many hours.

Author's Note

Trust is a powerful part of my business. I've always worked with clients in complete confidentiality, never discussing any of what I heard with anyone else. In this book, the stories are an amalgam of experiences that I've had coaching top-level executives over the past 25 years. Details have been changed to shield identities of both people and organisations, and, in many cases, stories have been blended. What matters is that the wisdom holds true.

Introduction:
What will I get out of this book?

'The way you see yourself shapes your life. How you define life determines your destiny. Your perspective will influence how you invest your time, spend your money, use your talents and value your relationships. We don't see things as they are, we see them as we are.'

Anais Nin

Leaders are operating under a microscope with every move called into question. In the course of more than 25 years spent coaching roughly 30,000 of the world's top chief executive officers (CEOs), senior executives and high-performing teams in more than 200 companies, I've never seen a more intense, pressure-filled time.

Clearly, leaders are looking for answers.

I learned early on that asking the right questions is the best way to help people find the right answers. The top level executives I work with don't need or want an extreme makeover. Indeed, most are successful, but – like top athletes – they recognise that they can always improve their game.

This book is packed with the key insights, battlefield lessons and wisdom I've gleaned from my unique position as confidant and coach to leaders of some of the world's best-known companies. I know what their problems are, and I'm hired to help solve them.

I encourage you to think of this book as a mirror. It's meant to be used as a launching pad to get you rocketing forward into the stratosphere of the best of the best.

In these pages, I'll share with you the lessons learned by others and the common pitfalls that I have seen over and over again in the world's boardrooms and executive suites. I'll also provide many practices and specifics that you can easily implement in your work and personal life.

You may have known the answers to many of the questions I pose in this book at one time in your career. What I often find in my one-on-one sessions, however, is that the certainty of those answers has been lost amid the frenetic pace of everyday work life.

The average CEO of a large corporation makes about £1.5 million annually. You cannot afford to have many wrong answers at that level. I can promise you that the investment you make in the self-examination that this book will spark will be well worth your time. Indeed, my clients typically report a 20 to 40 per cent saving of their time, and they credit our work with yielding at least 10 times their initial investment in coaching. You should be able to read this book in the course of a plane ride. I promise you that it will be time well spent.

What's life all about for you?

'**I** HAVE NEVER DISCUSSED THIS WITH anyone else.' I cannot count the number of times that sentence has come out of the mouths of CEOs and managing directors running multi-million-pound companies. Thus, I have spent many thousands of hours listening to the dreams, doubts, fears, strengths, weaknesses, difficulties, dilemmas and stresses of life at the top.

The key to self-development and operating at your peak is openness and honesty. The pent-up yearning for a confidant that I've encountered among executives leads me to believe that leaders rarely let their guards down – even with themselves.

To get the most out of this book, you'll have to work hard to complete the exercises and give serious thought to the questions I ask. Most importantly, you must strive to be completely honest in your answers – at the very least with yourself.

Million-dollar Question

> What are you hiding?

I've often found that people have areas of their lives that they simply choose to ignore – because they think the situations are hopeless or they are in denial or they are just plain too busy.

Sometimes we aren't even aware of the real issues we should be addressing in our lives. All of us have difficulty seeing ourselves clearly. In many cases, your blind spot is the critical block between the life you have and the one to which you aspire.

What are you avoiding looking at? What are you afraid to share? The sooner you get that topic on the table, the better. Here are some of the common issues leaders I have coached are grappling with and have been hesitant or fearful to address.

- The all-consuming nature of the job means that the rest of life is on hold – or worse.

- There's too little life outside work – common areas of concern are leaders' relationships with family, lack of fitness, love life.

- There's a tendency to feel insecurity and experience doubts about how they are viewed by others.

- Questions arise about how to sort out interpersonal difficulties on a team.

- Leaders feel they want to do something in the business but are shackled by commitments to shareholder value.

- There's the constant time pressure of a two- to three-year opportunity to 'make it'.

- Many are overly concerned about dealing with the media (feeling they ultimately can't win).

- What is the best use of their time? Where do they add the most value? Many feel they get sucked into lots of activities.

- There's often a wish to change the company culture, which isn't high-performing, but many do not know how.

- Those leaders who grew up in a non-technological age worry that they are not using technology effectively.

- Relationships with the boss, the company chairman or the board of directors can be problematical.

- Many worry about how they come across when they're working one on one or in a group, and how they compare with others in similar positions.

- Underperforming team members are often a problem – especially so if the poor performer is someone the leader has known a long time.

- Lack of people skills is another worry. How does this affect their leadership?

- Leaders often find it difficult to understand a new management style.

- What's the next career move? What is the leader to do after retirement?

- At the deepest level, it's a question of meaning: Life is going past in a blur, and leaders are completely exhausted and not that happy. Is it worth it?

All of these are important topics that require examination. However, they often go unaddressed for months or years, or they are never addressed at all – at dire cost to both business and personal lives.

Stop and Reflect _____

List the things that you have never discussed with complete openness and honesty with anyone. You may identify with the list above, or have other issues that you've kept to yourself. What is life all about for *you*?

Leadership Note: *It is lonely at the top.*

My work with leaders around the world has shown me that it *is* lonely at the top. Leaders rarely have a peer with whom they can be vulnerable within the organisation and are understandably loath to divulge sensitive issues to outsiders. The cold reality is that a senior leader has very few places to go to be completely open and honest.

Most of these topics are difficult – if not impossible – to discuss within an organisation, and you probably don't have anyone to go to within it even if you wanted to. Advisers, consultants, lawyers and partners at home may not understand the issues you are facing.

Once you reach the senior management level, in most organisations it's countercultural to admit even the tiniest problem or dilemma. The pressure is on to appear supremely confident with a can-do, positive attitude about every aspect of the business. Just flip through a few annual reports, and you'll see the positive spin at work. And if you think you are doing everything right, you are in a dangerous place.

Wake-up Call

Find someone to talk to.

No matter what level of leadership you're on, you need a peer, mentor or confidant whom you can trust implicitly. As you read the questions and exercises I give you in this book, you will get a good feel for what working with me as your coach is like. Great coaches don't tell people what to do. The world is full of people telling other people what to do or thinking they know what's right for others. The coaching relationship is about helping you see what's right for you, to discover what life is all about for *you* and to know what issues you should be addressing. My goal in writing this book is to help you find answers whether you do or don't currently have a confidant.

In conjunction with reading *Tales from the Top*, you might decide that having someone to discuss your discoveries and thoughts with would be useful. So how do you find someone to trust? You want someone with whom you can relax and be comfortable. That person, who should be non-judgemental, must offer the absolute integrity of confidentiality and understand your business realm and the demands of leadership. You want someone who is at peace in his or her own life and is skilful at helping you focus on what's important.

Ideally, your confidant or coach should be attuned to the fact that the presenting issue often isn't the real issue, or it doesn't represent the whole picture. A warning sign that you have the wrong coach or mentor is if you state a problem such as 'I'm having trouble managing my time' and you are given a snap solution. When a person jumps straight to a solution, that's a sign of inexperience. Instead, seek out someone willing to help you solve problems.

I would suggest recently retired CEOs, senior executives, coaches and consultants as possibilities. Internal confidants to consider would be the finance or human-resources director or a non-executive director on your board. Or, if you are on a less senior level, look for a peer or someone in the human-resources department.

The person must be a skilled listener. Be careful not to choose someone who is overly analytical. A person who is primarily left-brained will be tempted to impose what he or she believes are the right answers to your questions. A good coach ultimately helps you discover the answer within yourself. That's a big distinction.

Million-dollar Question

So what is life all about?

People often answer this critical question completely out of sync with the way they are living. Leaders usually talk about their loved ones as the most precious thing to them. Yet over and over again attending the business dinner takes precedence over a child's sporting activity. The habitual 80-hour (or more) working week and a string of broken promises to the family are evidence that points to a life that is out of line with the one that they claim to want.

Furthermore, you might be surprised to know that relatively few leaders have planned out their careers. For most, life happened and carried them along. So they are sacrificing their lives for careers that don't necessarily meet many of their wants and needs. Most of the thousands of leaders with whom I have worked had some general sense of their career goals, but that's different from strategically planning career progression. Many have been driven by financial reward and power, but ultimately found them hollow. Generally, even the most senior executives fail to pause and evaluate what they really want out of life until they are facing the end of their careers, and some don't even do it then.

Leadership Note: *Ask what is your purpose in life, and what you may have to do to achieve it.*

Once you allow yourself to explore what your purpose is in life, you might find that purpose requires small adjustments or enormous change.

A CEO of a large manufacturer with whom I was working expressed concern about one of her top executives, whom she had recently promoted to technical director – a vitally important post within the organisation. 'He's struggling in this job,' she told me.

He was so deep in denial, however, that he deflected any of her attempts to engage him about the problem she was seeing. 'I know there's something there, but I can't interpret the root cause. Does he not have enough people to help him? Is there trouble at home? I just don't know. Can you try to get beyond the surface?'

When I first met him, he was working incredibly long hours implementing a new information-technology system. 'I'm already working unacceptable hours, and they're about to go up,' he said in our first session.

At the outset of a new coaching relationship, I often ask my clients to go through a standard five-hour profile – a comprehensive mix of life interviews and a series of psychometric tests – with a psychologist. Then the psychologist writes up an extensive psychological report, which we go through with the person. In this case, I had never seen a profile so inappropriate to the job the man had. He was a square peg in a round hole, and, after examining the profile results, I was surprised he'd even got that far in the company. Clearly, here was a man who didn't know what life was all about for him.

What I had to address with him was blatantly obvious to me: he was working too many hours, and he was under huge stress because he was overwhelmed in his role. In fact, his wife wasn't speaking to him, and he rarely saw his kids. 'My observation from listening to you is that two things in your life are completely out of kilter,' I said at our next session. 'First, you're working an unacceptable number of hours. But more importantly, according to the psychologist, you're in a job that isn't suited to you.'

Wake-up Call

Be sure you're asking yourself the right questions.

When we started the coaching relationship, my client wasn't asking the right question. He wasn't asking, 'Should I be doing this job at all?' He was asking, 'How do I cope?'

I redirected the questions he was asking himself: 'Is this job worth the emotional toll it's taking on my family? Do I really want this job?' Like so many of us, he was so immersed in the task at hand that he had not allowed himself to step back and take an objective overview of his path.

I discovered through our coaching sessions that he came from a family where the only prized value was to succeed in business. His early programming was to believe that his only worth came from how much money he made and how big his role was in business. Throughout his career, he never asked himself, 'Given who I am, is the corporate world the best choice for me?' That question arises again: what is life all about for him?

At the end of our coaching sessions, the net result was that he left the company and moved to the mountains, because he loved the outdoors. He and his wife started an adventure company – taking clients on nature hikes in the summer, and snowshoeing and sledging in the winter. A good strategic thinker, he brought his business acumen to bear on their tiny entrepreneurial venture. He gave up a big salary and left a job working for a top corporation. By most people's standards, he ditched an enviable position. Although he earned far less money working in his little enterprise in the rural mountain town with only his wife for support, he was happier.

By facing the truth that he was living out someone else's expectations for his life and exercising the courage to act on that revelation, this man ultimately answered the larger question that all of us should address and the title of this chapter: 'What's life all about for you?' In his case, it was about following his heart rather than doing what he'd been conditioned to believe he should be doing.

Million-dollar Question

What are you afraid of?

A recent study of Fortune 1000 CEOs revealed that their number-one motivator – at 43 per cent – was fear (power came in a distant second at 22 per cent, followed by money at 7 per cent). Based on my work, the study results did not surprise me. The fear in many executive offices is almost palpable.

The managing partner of one of the world's leading audit practices brought me in to coach him and other senior partners on how to lead offices more effectively. A survey of his own staff revealed that his leadership was weak. In our first three meetings, he was formal and guarded. Nonetheless, I detected a sense of weariness. I asked, 'How long have you been leading the office?'

'Seven years,' he replied.

'How long do you plan to continue?'

'Indefinitely.'

'Is that the norm?'

'No, normally this role is a five-year tenure, but I still have more that I want to accomplish.' I made a note of that bit of information to return to later.

He attributed being beyond his tenure to the lack of a successor. 'Why don't we work on identifying a successor for you?' I asked (not having a successor in a global business is a common problem). He agreed to a goal of identifying a successor within the next year. I knew, however, that something more than the lack of a successor was behind his refusal to move on from his role, and added, 'Let's revisit the topic of your future at a later date.'

By our third session, he let his guard down. 'Do you enjoy your role as leader of the office?' I asked.

He paused, and then replied, 'I enjoyed it the first five years, but I'm very tired. I know I'm not the greatest leader in the world, but I've done my best. I'm not sure I've got the energy.'

'Why do you feel compelled to soldier on, then?' I asked.

He paused and then answered, 'When my job was auditing, I always feared I wasn't as bright as the other auditors and that sooner or later my peers or our clients would find that out. Now, that fear has been compounded by another fear. In the seven years that I've been in this office, our business has moved on. If I give up this position, I'm certain to be found lacking.'

Like all industries, his had changed a bit, but certainly nobody would have imagined that he felt like a fraud. After all, here was a talented, powerful man leading a global business with hundreds of employees. His insecurity was the real issue, but, since he had nobody to talk to about it, he had been paralysed by his fear.

> **Leadership Note:** *Fear is often the biggest block when it comes to answering the key question of what life is all about for you.*

In this case, this man suffered from what is called impostor syndrome. He spent his life in absolute dread that he would be found out and labelled incompetent. Psychologists would say that early parental conditioning comes into play. As we talked, I wasn't surprised to learn that he came from a home where nothing was ever good enough.

As a youngster, one of the world's top tennis players, once brought home the runner-up's trophy from a tournament. His father threw it in the bin. That's not an easy one to overcome.

I had to help this managing partner see that he was capable. Only then was he willing to move on to the next role.

Stop and Reflect

Dig deep and ferret out your darkest thoughts. Write down the one thing that scares you the most about your current situation. This exercise is all part of finding the answer to the question of what life is really all about for you.

Wake-up Call

**Get rid of the fear in your life, so you will
truly be free to live the life you've imagined.**

Fear strangles greatness. Until you learn to conquer fear in your life, you won't be able to sort out the answers you seek. When you examine what you are afraid of, often you will find that your fears aren't based in reality. Once you express your fears, you'll often find that they lose power over you. There is freedom in asking for help in dealing with a fear.

One CEO believed that his fear of public speaking was hindering his ability to lead his company. Part of what deepened his panic about speaking in public was that he wasn't comfortable with the traditional methods speakers are told to use. Once he talked about his problem with his wife and a few close associates, he gradually established a routine of preparing for a big speech that worked for him. To outsiders, his method looked unorthodox, but what mattered was the results. His ability to communicate to large groups grew to be his strength. Again, what's important is figuring out what works for you.

When a US company took over a Swiss pharmaceutical firm, the management consultancy that the US firm used to assess whether the acquisition made good strategic sense suggested that the new CEO chat with me since I'd worked with numerous European companies. Bright, energetic, and a Harvard Business School graduate with wide experience of different nationalities, this CEO had every reason to be completely confident in his new role.

I never assume, however. I asked, 'You come across as capable and experienced. Confidentially, do you have any fears or anxieties about this role?' At the outset, he said he felt fine. 'Is there anything about taking over a Swiss company that gives you any cause for questioning or anxiety?'

He paused and said, 'Are you sure this isn't going any further?' Satisfied that he was safe, he continued: 'I've never understood the Swiss.'

'What do you mean?'

'In the United States, we have a reasonably straightforward culture. People say what they mean. With the Swiss, you have to read between the lines. They are reserved, and there's a subtlety to the communication here. My fear is that I'll come in with my typical open, honest style and that will put people off. Do I need to adapt my style?'

This concern was difficult to admit, because he had broad international experience and thought he should be able to cope wherever he was. His fear of making a cultural blunder was an important thing to get on the table. Once he revealed his worry, we developed strategies to assure his success in his new role. He called a meeting with the executive team of the company his own had just acquired and told the team about his concern over the cultural differences. He asked them to let him know if he was coming off as too brusque or confrontational. His openness accomplished two things: it eased his mind and quickly won his new team over to him.

> **Leadership Note:** *Just giving voice to your concern goes a long way to easing anxiety.*

A woman who headed up the legal department for a US-based telecommunications firm had been divorced for many years. She had no children and had dedicated her life to work. Then, suddenly, she met a man with whom she fell in love. She worried that a relationship would get in the way of work and was anxious about what a change might mean. She simply needed somebody to share her news with. After talking through the situation, she felt free to pursue the relationship.

> **Leadership Note:** *Everyone – even a top performer – needs help now and then.*

Leaders often stumble when faced with something they think they ought to know. A superstar, senior-level executive in a business divided into five regions had responsibility for the Americas. A former basketball star on the collegiate level, he had a big frame with a big presence to match. When he came into a room, he commanded it and always appeared completely confident.

Over the years, headhunters called him constantly. A global retail chain approached him, offering a plum position. As we talked through whether or not he should take the role, I became aware that there was something he wasn't saying about this situation. So I probed. 'Is there anything that worries you about the move?' I asked.

Somewhat sheepishly and with great difficulty, he said, 'I know it sounds pathetic, but I don't know how to play the offer.'

'What do you mean?'

'I've never changed jobs, so I don't know the process,' he explained, obviously relieved. 'Should I get an employment lawyer to negotiate the deal for me? I'm not sure what to ask for in my remuneration package.'

Once his concern was out in the open, it was an easy fix. We discussed how to find a good employment lawyer and what his expectations should be. Ultimately, he took the CEO role.

Wake-up Call

Don't let pride keep you from asking for help.

When a US furniture manufacturer fell on hard times, the long-time CEO who had been in place for many years was fired. The board went through a lengthy, tortuous process of deciding whether to bring in a candidate from the outside or pull someone from within. For some time, I had been coaching one of the three internal candidates, a man with close to 30 years in the company.

Picking the right leader was a difficult decision for the board. If it went outside, the CEO would have to go through a steep learning curve. The first year, the person would be learning about and adjusting to a big, new role; the second, getting to grips with it; and only in the third would the outsider really begin to add value. The board was concerned over whether it could afford that learning curve when the business was in such trouble. Finally, after much agonising, the board chose the internal candidate whom I was coaching, largely because of his long experience in the company. The assumption was that he knew the business, so he was the best person to dig the company out of this hole.

Now our coaching sessions became about how he could be most effective in his new CEO role. We'd had two sessions since he'd taken the new position. He was working longer and longer hours, was looking more stressed and wasn't enjoying his position. Previously, he had been positive and effective, so I noticed a real change. But in our sessions he didn't talk about the long hours and the stress. I suspected that might be an issue and had checked with his personal assistant. (I often get permission to speak to others in the organisation from the person I'm coaching. A leader's team and support staff often have a much clearer view of what's going on than the leader.) She said, 'His schedule is completely insane.'

During a discussion about something unrelated to the frantic pace he was keeping, I stopped the conversation and said, 'With respect, I don't want to continue this conversation. I want you to tell me honestly: how are you feeling?'

That simple question stopped him cold. He thought about it for a few moments and then replied, 'I haven't admitted this to anyone else, because I am fearful it would have a de-motivational effect on people, but I will answer you honestly. I've been in this business for thirty years. I thought I knew everything about this business and that I'd be able to succeed in this role. That's why I took it on. But I want to tell you that it's ten times harder than I could ever have imagined. I'm not at all sure I can succeed.' He was very emotional. As with so many leaders, the burden of portraying to everybody else that he was confident and on top of everything only added to his stress.

Once he finally revealed the heart of the matter, he was relieved. More importantly, we could get into a much more useful conversation and dig into the different aspects of what was so hard. 'Let's bring your top team in and engage in a much more authentic conversation about the business and about where you're struggling,' I suggested.

He called a meeting and told his team, 'I need your support and help.' He laid out the thorniest issues he was facing and got a lot of great feedback. That was a significant moment that led to a much more effective year than he would otherwise have had. In time, the business began to turn around and that led to an orderly transition a year later, when he decided to leave. His honesty gave him the freedom to make that choice on good terms. He is now in the business of helping other leaders as an executive coach.

Stop and Reflect

At times you may need more than one coach or confidant because you require someone with special knowledge.

A good coach or confidant must be clear on what they *can't* help with as well as what they can. When a British CEO was chosen to lead a large, successful Scottish manufacturing company, I worked with him during his first hundred days in the new role. What life was all about for him was about to change: the unknown beckoned. In our sessions he told me that he needed to get a real understanding of Scotland's culture, norms and values, both in society as a whole and within the business culture.

I had worked quite a lot in the country where he was now leading a business, but I couldn't claim to understand it fully. Obviously, he needed somebody in addition to me to understand the people and the culture. But neither of us had any idea who that person should be. 'Should it be a person in the business you are going to?' I asked.

We decided that wouldn't work, because most people in the business were young. What he needed was an elder statesman who was more of a peer. Also, his focus needed to be on strategy and business objectives in the first three months. If he used an internal confidant there was a danger that too much focus would be on conversations on the culture rather than the task at hand.

'Is there somebody *within* the business you can ask regarding whom to use *outside* the business as a confidant?' I asked. He decided to go to the human-resources director, who recommended a senior executive who was well connected politically in the culture and who led another business that, like the company my client was now leading, was a significant plank in Scotland's economy.

This man readily agreed to serve in that capacity because he was at a stage in life where he wanted to be a mentor. And, because he was well connected within upper echelons, his altruistic nature came into play, because he knew it was important to the economy for the new CEO to succeed. The new CEO met with the elder statesman a number of times, and he was instrumental in helping him understand the nuances of both the country's culture and the business culture.

In another case, a young entrepreneur who had grown a substantial transportation company was about to take his enterprise public. We agreed that it was important for him to find someone who had been through that process. I set up an initial lunch meeting with a former client who had taken his company public to see whether they connected. They were intellectually stimulated by each other and launched into a three-year mentoring relationship.

Wake-up Call

Look for a mutually rewarding mentoring relationship in order to increase your self-knowledge.

So what's in it for you as an unpaid mentor? Consider making yourself available as a confidant because you'll likely find it personally satisfying to help somebody else who is in a situation you've encountered. There also might be a synergy between your two businesses. A good mentor recognises that he or she frequently learns from the person being mentored. In my own life, I serve as a mentor to half a dozen or so coaches who are less experienced. I learn from them constantly, because they bring fresh eyes to coaching.

Million-dollar Question

Are you willing to dare to be open?

A 33-year-old man at a leading global accountancy firm was a real high flier and appeared to be on track to become a senior partner. A Warwick Business School graduate, a former Olympic athlete and tirelessly ambitious, he was hugely successful with clients. In our coaching sessions, he was questioning how quickly he would ascend to the position of senior partner and be appointed to the global strategy council. He'd been offered a job outside the business as a CEO, and the offer was very tempting to him.

'Obviously, to evaluate this situation properly, you need to talk to someone within your firm to find out your prospects,' I said. 'Who can you trust?'

'Nobody,' he said. 'I'll be viewed as too impatient and presumptuous, especially given my age. You're just expected to do your best, and sooner or later you'll get promoted.' He went on to explain that the ethos was that, since the company was so wonderful, why would one consider leaving?

'Worse,' he continued, 'I'll be seen as disloyal and uncommitted. Having that conversation would be shooting myself in the foot.'

Stop and Reflect

Let people know what you are really thinking – even when it's scary.

I pushed and challenged, but he cited one or two of his predecessors who had previously taken that step, and it had negatively affected their careers. Ultimately, he kept quiet and decided to take the outside job. When he announced his resignation, the senior partners were absolutely horrified about losing this great talent. The truth was that his promotion was in the works. After the fact, they even tried to dissuade him from leaving, but by then he had set his course.

I felt badly for both parties. His impatience and unwillingness to take a chance by waiting cost him a job he'd been striving for, and having a culture where employees felt unable to voice concerns and dreams cost the company dearly.

Wake-up Call

Step out on faith and go for the win–win.

Another coach called me and said that he had a client with whom he thought I could do a better job, because I tend to challenge conventional thinking. Married and 43 years old, this woman had recently been named CEO of a major do-it-yourself retail company. When I arrived at her office for our first session, however, I was struck by the fact that pictures of electronics – not do-it-yourself products – covered the walls of her office. She clearly loved the high-tech world. 'Tell me about your job,' I said upon our first meeting.

'I hate it.'

It was an interesting start.

As it turns out, this woman had been one of two internal candidates whom the entrepreneur who owned both ventures had considered for the role of CEO of his high-flying electronics company. My client was angry and resentful when the job went to her peer. In her current role at the DIY retail chain, she believed she had been demoted and relegated to a lesser role. Now my client was driven by the desire to 'show him he made the wrong choice'.

Formerly, she had done a good job, was close to the entrepreneur, and was happily ensconced in an exciting, fun, smart office. She dreamed of proving to her boss how good she was by making the struggling chain a success and getting invited back into the fold.

Stop and Reflect

Face the facts of your situation.

I've rarely seen a client succeed for long when the primary driver is negative, but getting her to see that would take some work. 'How easy will it be to succeed at this position?' I asked.

'Very difficult,' she said.

'Suppose the entrepreneur did invite you back. What job would you like?'

She named the job she didn't get last time.

'How long do you think it will be before that job comes up again?'

She estimated four years at the earliest.

'If I were a betting man, what are the odds – one out of ten – in four years' time you'll be wildly successful in this job you hate, and the entrepreneur will invite you back to do a job for which he has already passed you over once?' I asked.

She glumly agreed the odds were slim to none.

'What does your husband say?' I asked.

'He thinks I'm crazy working here,' she said. 'He sees me unhappy and thinks I'm capable of a lot more.'

We had dinner that evening, and her husband joined us. When a person is facing a tough issue, I sometimes find it useful to meet the partner or life partner. If I don't see the couple together, I will typically ask my client how he or she believes their partner sees things. Those who love us most often have a good read on our lives. In contrast to her his wife – stiff and formal in a grey skirt suit and white shirt – her husband was a gentle, cheerful, artsy sort of person. 'She'll never leave,' he said. 'She's going to die on her sword to make this work.'

> **Leadership Note:** *Deal with negative feelings head-on. Simmering resentment and anger are lethal to living your life on the highest plane.*

She could not move on to the next step until she had dealt with her resentment towards her boss. I asked, 'What could you do about your resentment?'

'I could have a conversation with him and tell him how upset and disappointed I was not to get the job,' she said. 'I never understood how he could have picked the other person.'

Then she added, 'I'd also tell him how much I miss daily business contact with him. I never see him now. Those were the best times of my life.'

She set up a meeting with the entrepreneur right away. The entrepreneur said two important things in that meeting. First, he told her that it had been an excruciating decision, because both candidates were great. Second, because he had to fill two jobs, he thought my client had the best chance at turning the troubled chain around, because she was stronger strategically.

Knowing that the entrepreneur's decision had been a close call – and, furthermore, that he had given my client what he saw as the tougher assignment because he admired her strategic thinking – was a revelation. When the woman said he had missed contact with him, the entrepreneur said, 'Let me think about that.' A week later, he called my client with a special three-month project dealing with the electronics business that required her to report directly to the entrepreneur.

Only after she'd dealt with her hurt, anger and confusion from being passed over for the job of her dreams could my client look to the future. 'Given that you've admitted you have only a one-in-ten chance of getting this job when and if it opens up again, you need to start to think about getting something else,' I said at our next coaching session.

She wasn't, however, ready to be in the hunt.

'Why don't you make it a goal to speak to two people a week in your personal network and see if anything emerges?' I suggested. She agreed.

Two months later, she rang me up very excited and bubbly. She had landed an interview to be chief operating officer of a major electronics company. If she got the job, she would be promoted to CEO in nine months. I'd done some work for the company and happened to know the person interviewing her, so I was able to offer my perspective on the woman I was coaching.

She got the job.

Wake-up Call

A problem shared is a problem halved.

For three years, I coached the senior executives in a company where the CEO was highly visible. Whenever I suggested he engage in a coaching relationship, he always agreed that it would be valuable, but he never followed through.

After observing me on many occasions, he finally agreed to an exploratory meeting. I explained to him that my clients always decide where the boundaries are. I said, 'I will push up against the boundaries if an issue is impacting your work life, but, if you don't want to talk about it, we won't.'

Once he realised he was in the driver's seat regarding the agenda, he was reassured and agreed to start coaching on business issues. At one point he stated, 'My personal life is difficult,' and left it at that. He put a clear boundary around what we would talk about and what we wouldn't. I left the door slightly ajar so that if at any stage he wanted to go into any other areas, we could.

Million-dollar Question

What are you avoiding looking at?

We developed a useful agenda around questions about how long he would continue in his role, who his successor would be and how much time he would spend as an ambassador for the company. When we got into the topic of how long he was staying in that role and who his successor was, we bumped up against his personal situation. By that stage he felt safe enough with me to confide that he was a widower with a severely disabled child in his teens. 'I have very little support in caring for my son, and I worry about what will happen to him once I'm gone,' he said.

Stop and Reflect

Identify the one area of your life that appears almost impossible to change. It's that aspect of your life you find yourself unwilling to examine. Is it a relationship? Your physical state?

Although he longed to leave that business and thought one year was a good timetable, he was concerned about his financial future.

He wondered whether he could get another job with as good a package as the one he had and that would offer as much freedom as he had enjoyed in his current role. He had set up his position so that he could work a great deal from home in order to be available for his son.

Once he stopped avoiding the real issue, which he felt was hopeless and had no hope of changing, and we talked it through, he could see his financial worry was not valid. With his stellar track record, it was highly likely he'd be able to get a better remuneration package, and, if a company wanted him enough, that company would certainly give him some flexibility with his schedule. I pointed out that, even if that freedom to work from home couldn't be replicated, an increased remuneration package would allow him to put a good plan in place for his son's continued care. Sure enough, he landed an even better position that answered all his concerns and desires.

Wake-up Call

Be open to solutions that you've never considered.

Clients often feel pressure to make big decisions on someone else's time frame. However, when the decision is going to affect your life and that of your family in a big way, pausing to make sure you've considered all the angles is a wise course. When you're under the gun to make a decision, you may overlook the best solution.

A good example of this common pitfall was with the CEO of a large steel manufacturer. A former air force pilot, this archetypical fighting man had operated behind enemy lines. His background meant that he was used to making quick, clear decisions and acting on them immediately. In his experience as a leader, being indecisive could literally cost him his life and the lives of his crews.

He had become one of my best and most committed clients after a rocky start. The human-resources director had proposed my services to him, and he was clearly sceptical about his need for a coach. I knew he was wondering how someone on the outside could help him. He grudgingly agreed to meet me, largely to get the HR person off his back. I asked him to give me an hour, and he saw I could mix it with him. Once he decided coaching was valuable, he threw himself into the process 100 per cent, and I coached him in many areas.

One year after our last session, he called me out of the blue: 'I want to use you as a sounding board,' he said, sounding urgent.

'Would you like to tell me in advance of our session what we'll be discussing?'

'The company is selling out, and I have to decide whether to leave the business or to stay with the new owner,' said the 55-year-old, who had remarried and had two school-age children to consider. 'The acquiring company wants to know my decision.'

He had it set up in his mind that he had only two choices: (1) leave now; (2) commit to the acquiring company, and keep doing the job with new management. He had carved out two hours for our discussion and fully expected it to end with the decision made. He never delayed or dithered about a decision.

I pointed out that he had a third choice: 'Decide not to decide. It will take at least nine months for the deal to go through. Use the time to observe the new owners and work on negotiations. Sometimes you can choose not to make a decision and that's a decision itself.'

That was a breakthrough moment for him. He had a paradigm shift and saw how a conscious decision not to decide for now was a tactical decision. Over the next nine months he gathered more data to make such an important life decision. He ultimately decided to stay on.

Million-dollar Question

Would you rather have the results you want in life, or the reasons you haven't got them?

Many of us are stuck in the face of issues, problems and dilemmas because we see them as one large piece. We get paralysed, because the issue looks too big – too big to get our arms around, too big to deal with. I have yet to see any issue, problem or situation in corporate life or life outside where a clear-headed, dispassionate look at what the individual could do – however small – to move a situation forward has not elicited at least one action step. Figuring out the first action step moves the individual from a problem state to a process state – from stuck to unstuck.

Stop and Reflect

Consider taking bite-sized chunks. Pick your most intractable problem and identify one step, however small, that you could take today to move it forward. You may be able to change the question 'What's life all about for me?' to 'How's life changing for me?'

In 1961, John F. Kennedy made his famous statement, 'I believe that this nation should commit itself to achieving the goal, before this decade is out, of landing a man on the moon and returning him safely to Earth.' Many, including most people in the space business, saw the goal he laid out as impossible. But, through a process of countless bite-sized chunks by a committed team of people, that goal – which had seemed ridiculously optimistic – was achieved.

> **Leadership Note:** *The longest journey starts with the first step.*

Congratulations! By reading this chapter, you've hopefully taken that important first step towards the life you've imagined.

Wake-up Call

Take action today.

Executive Summary

Million-dollar Questions

- What are you hiding?

- So what is life all about?

- What are you afraid of?

- Are you willing to dare to be open?

- What are you avoiding looking at?

- Would you rather have the results you want in life, or the reasons you haven't got them?

Stop and Reflect

- List the things that you have never discussed with complete openness and honesty with anyone. What is life all about for *you*?

- Dig deep and ferret out your darkest thoughts. Write down the one thing that scares you the most about your current situation.

- At times you may need more than one coach or confidant because you require someone with special knowledge.

- Let people know what you are really thinking – even when it's scary.

- Face the facts of your situation.

- Identify the one area of your life that appears almost impossible to change.

- Consider taking bite-sized chunks. Pick your most intractable problem and identify one step, however small, that you could take today to move it forward. You may be able to change the question 'What's life all about for me?' to 'How's life changing for me?

Wake-up Calls

- Find someone to talk to.

- Be sure you're asking yourself the right questions.

- Get rid of the fear in your life, so you will truly be free to live the life you've imagined.

- Don't let pride keep you from asking for help.

- Look for a mutually rewarding mentoring relationship in order to increase your self-knowledge.

- Step out on faith and go for the win–win.

- A problem shared is a problem halved.

- Be open to solutions that you've never considered.

- Take action today.

Leadership Notes

- It *is* lonely at the top.

- Ask what is your purpose in life, and what you may have to do to achieve it.

- Fear is often the biggest block when it comes to answering the key question of what life is all about for you.

- Just giving voice to your concern goes a long way to easing anxiety.

- Everyone – even a top performer – needs help now and then.

- Deal with negative feelings head-on. Simmering resentment and anger are lethal to living your life on the highest plane.

- The longest journey starts with the first step.

Who are you, and who do others say you are?

WE LIVE IN AN ETHOS of *doing*, not *being*. We equate success with doing, doing, doing – continually adding to our long list of accomplishments. Shockingly, many high-level people have to-do lists for relaxing – goals for what they want to accomplish during their time 'off'. And they are just as manic about their weekend schedules as they are about the working week.

I find it tremendously ironic that relatively few leaders feel free to operate their own businesses and personal lives on a timetable of their choosing.

The master attributes of high-performing leaders and teams are clarity and a high level of self-awareness. The most successful CEOs and leaders I've encountered are self-reflective. Because they are committed to continuous improvement on a personal level, they allow themselves the luxury of slowing down and thinking carefully about how they come across to people. They ask questions such as: What is it that I'm doing that's not as effective as it could be?

Million-dollar Question

What knowledge about yourself are you missing that could make a significant difference in your life and/or your company's performance?

Top-performing leaders seek out honest feedback. They genuinely want to know whether their interactions help or hinder the performance of those around them. On the opposite end of the spectrum are leaders who are frightened of what they would hear.

Most leaders fall squarely in the middle. They don't give any thought to feedback, because they don't see any real value in it. Indeed, the basic performance management disciplines of clear objectives and periodic reviews are often missing or sketchy at the top of organisations. Beyond the token annual review, which – based on my experience – is perfunctory, poorly executed and too infrequent to be of real use, scant attention is paid to giving or getting feedback. And a process for delivering all-important 360-degree feedback is nonexistent.

Unfortunately, leaders rarely ask for feedback. Most assume that because they've made it to the top, or got pretty close, they are fine, thank you very much. And, if there are any problems with the way they are, they leave it up to everybody else to work around their management style. A relatively small percentage of leaders are willing to put in the hard work required to make lasting changes and sustainable improvements.

Just as ironically, leaders think they give feedback all the time, and they also think they are good at it. Ask them and that's what they will tell you. Their own people, however, will give you a different story. They will say the top leaders never give feedback. For example, if I am coaching the chief financial officer in a company, the CEO will give me that person's strengths and weaknesses. When I subsequently ask the CFO, 'How do you think the CEO views you?' invariably the person replies, 'I'm not sure.' If they were given feedback at all, it was fuzzy to them and, therefore, not particularly useful.

Wake-up Call

Task, task, task. Do, do, do. No review.
If this sounds like the rhythm of your day,
this chapter is vital for you.

I was coaching a top executive of an international accounting firm. An important piece of the puzzle was getting feedback from his boss, so that I could be more effective in our sessions. When I called for a time to discuss this key executive, his boss's assistant said, 'I can give you fifteen minutes in five weeks' time.'

I was incredulous and asked, 'You're certain he doesn't have any time in his schedule before then?'

'There are no other open slots.'

I went back to my client and said, 'I'm sorry, but I'm having difficulty getting your assessment completed. Could you put in a call and smooth the way?'

'I can't get him on the phone either, and he's my boss,' my client replied.

To top it all, the assistant phoned the day before my appointed fifteen-minute slot. 'Sorry, but he's had to cancel,' she said, barely pausing for a breath. 'I'll print out your email and ask him your questions in my next meeting with him.'

Not even having fifteen minutes to spare in five weeks to discuss how to help one of your top executives implies enormous stress on that individual and a maniacal business pace. He'd left no gaps for thinking, no gaps for dealing with the unforeseen. As the leader of the company, this relentlessly task-focused CEO was setting a tone throughout the business, and it wasn't a good one.

The latest badge of honour in business is to be constantly busy and to be difficult to meet with. That supposedly validates how important you are. I've observed, however, that the more senior you are, the more time you should spend strategically thinking. And, in order to see the big picture, you've got to tune in to yourself, your family and friends, your people and your customers.

Stop and Reflect

Consider the type of person you are. List key questions about yourself and try to answer them. Then get honest answers from those around you – your life partner, your personal assistant, a trusted adviser, and select employees in the company. How do their answers compare with yours?

Here are some sample questions to get you started:

- Where do I focus my time and energy?

- How do others see me?

- What needs are not being met in my business life and in my personal life?

- What are the things I ought to be doing to add the most value to the business?

- What in my leadership elicits top performance from employees, and what stifles it?

- Am I aware of the needs/wants of those around me?

Wake-up Call

Don't let too much depend on you.

'When you were 25,' I said to the creative director of a big US advertising agency, 'where did you dream you'd be at this age?' She was 42.

'Right here,' she said. 'This job. This company.'

A dream come true? Hardly. The agency's new CEO was much tougher as a boss. The departure of several key clients kept her in a pressure cooker. And at home her husband, who had an equally demanding job that often kept him on the road, and her two pre-teen sons baulked at her additional hours. I wondered who listened and helped her unwind.

'No one, really. I have to keep careful boundaries with my colleagues.'

One benefit of coaching is that it thaws isolation.

We dug into issues on two fronts: how to relate to the new CEO and how not to be consumed by her work. She wasn't optimistic, but it was still her dream job. She felt extra pressure, however, because she was her family's major breadwinner (her husband was in sales and had an erratic pay schedule). A very large bonus cheque nine months hence would pay off their mortgage. She was willing to give it a go.

We started with the CEO-related issues. While she always understood what the previous CEO wanted, the new executive was an enigma. She couldn't read whether he approved of her work, knew what she was doing or had any notion of her perspective or strategy. As we talked, she was surprised to realise how little she communicated with him.

'How about setting up a three-month review?' I suggested. 'Give him a chance to tell you what he thinks about your work – and show him what you're made of. Now, is he the kind of boss who needs to know the agenda in advance?'

She thought he might be and emailed him the questions:

- Where have I succeeded and how have I disappointed?

- What works and what doesn't work in our relationship?

- What changes should I make?

- Overall, how am I doing?

During our next coaching session, she told me that the CEO expressed delight with her work and that they had established a good start to their working relationship. We moved on to the matter of how her work consumed her.

'I can't imagine not being immersed,' she said.

'Can you imagine where you'll be in a year? You've gone forward unchanged, got your bonus, it's a year later – now tell me how it's been.'

She paused, thinking. 'It's been awful. I've lost so much more time with my sons. Things are more harried than ever in our family life. And nothing else has happened in my life except this job.'

'Any ideas about what to change?'

'No.'

I invited her to brainstorm with me, and asked her a series of questions:

- What have you thought about doing but dismissed as not feasible?

- What would you do if you were braver?

- If you could do anything to resolve your current predicament, what would it be?

- What would you do with an unlimited budget?

- If your boss could do something to get you out of this dilemma, what would it be?

- Of all the executives you've known, who managed work and life most effectively? What would that person tell you to do right now?

- If you learned that this was the last year of your life and if you still wanted to work, what would you do?

- If you suddenly found yourself running the company, what would you do?

The rapid-fire brainstorming led into thoughtful review. Two completely new ideas popped out of the list. The first was to recruit a number two. While a hiring freeze precluded bringing on a new employee, she could make a case for returns exceeding costs and recruit among existing employees. The second idea was to negotiate a four-day working week: work from home, reconnect with her family, get just as much accomplished, and be happier.

> **Leadership Note:** *Know thyself – and let thyself be known.*

She was ecstatic. Then the smile faded. 'It won't happen,' she said.

'OK, my creative dynamo. Go to work. You love the ideas. Now write them up and sell them. Make the case for change.'

'They won't take it seriously. They'll say I'm just another hysterical woman crying for help.'

'You've been too competent for too long for them to say that. Make the case, because the worst thing that can happen is an intolerable year that ends with a huge bonus, which settles your mortgage and puts your sons through college. So give it your best shot.'

She was amazed when the company agreed to a flexitime plan. She had to complete several projects before it began, and it was only a three-month trial. But it was a win. She was also surprised to learn the CEO considered it unfortunate that she didn't already have a number two. 'Too much depends on you,' he told her. She thought she was doing everybody a favour by holding the fort all by herself.

She had been trapped there. And now she was climbing out. Later on she did hire a very competent number two.

Wake-up Call

Take time to be clear about your wants,
your needs, your strengths, your weaknesses.

The pressure on leaders to perform near to perfection is immense. It's a horrific strain to have to appear on top of your game all the time. The only way you can evolve into the best performer you can be is to talk about doubts, fears and screw-ups. Ironically, you get better and better when you expose your failures. Dialogue helps manage the pressure. It's part of the process of knowing who you are and who others say you are.

A corporate lawyer who was an international mergers and acquisitions (M&A) expert was extremely competent and recognised for it. Best of all, she loved her job. So, naturally, she was offered a promotion. Instead of the niche speciality she adored, now she would step up to managing a large legal department with responsibility for inside legal counsel in several countries where her company maintained offices. It was a major promotion, with more money, more responsibility, and a much broader role. How could she refuse?

She was learning to manage the much larger staff. As her coach, I had to ask, 'Is this the right job for you?' I think it's hard to succeed in a job you don't want in the first place, and I sensed her ambivalence.

'It's true that I miss the work of my last job,' she told me, 'and I'm like a fish out of water managing all these people. But I'm determined to play my part. I'll make this work.'

Bravely, she soldiered on, but the increasing unhappiness was evident. Even her husband observed that she was having less fun, working longer hours and becoming increasingly stressed. She wasn't doing what she *wanted* to do.

Stop and Reflect

Write down three roles you've had in your career where you've been most satisfied. Does your current role look like any of the three that you wrote down?

After nine months, I decided to play hardball. 'Look, you have three choices. You can persevere indefinitely, and, even though it hasn't happened so far, you might eventually learn to love this job as much as the last one. Your second option is to commit to exiting this job at a future point if you don't feel more positive about it. And your third choice? Leave now.'

We revisited why she agreed to take the promotion to begin with – more money, more responsibility, that sense of needing to play her part for the company. Then I asked her, given the range of possibilities she faced, what she really wanted.

'I want my old job back.'

'Why?'

'Because I love doing it, and I'm good at it.'

Once she voiced her unhappiness, the person whom she felt compelled to help out by accepting the job admitted that he had seen how my client was struggling and regretted promoting her to that role. Two years later, successfully back in her previous position, my client described herself as 'a round peg in a round hole with a smile on my face'.

That's the right fit.

Wake-up Call

**When your life is driven by 'shoulds'
and 'must-dos' you are in danger of
losing your genuine self.**

CEOs often imagine that they have to fit a certain mould when there are actually many different leadership styles. The chief operating officer of a large publicly held construction company got feedback from his staff that he was an impatient, unapproachable command-and-control leader. Yet, when they saw him with his wife and children, they were surprised to see he was completely different – loving, relaxed and funny.

Rather than simply deal with the symptom, which was his impatience, I asked him about the contrast between who he was at home and who he was on the job. He said that in business he needed to be 'tough'. Toughness, however, didn't come naturally to him – he had to work to maintain the uncomfortable, unpleasant façade. That's probably why he came across as impatient and frustrated.

> **Leadership Note:** *Be more true to yourself in your business. Don't try to be something you are not.*

Until he saw that his long-held belief in a tough business approach was wrong, he couldn't make a lasting change in his behaviour. Once he made that breakthrough, he became much more patient and empathetic with his staff – behaviour that was sustainable.

Many CEOs don't realise how damaging that 'tough' style can be on people. They fail to recognise their power and the diminishing effect their harsh stance has on people who are less confident or are new to the organisation.

Million-dollar Question

What is the effect of your leadership style? Does it state who you are – both to you and to others? And does it tell you how others see you?

Lots of businesses claim to have 360-degree feedback processes, but those processes have little value because they are too general and tell people what they already know. Feedback forms often don't work, because people rarely feel truly free to be honest on the written page. Besides, if you're simply looking at a checklist, you'll have to do too much guesswork regarding the feedback. For example, what if someone ticks a box that says you are 'poor at meeting management'. What does that really mean? Do you fail to start on time? Are you frequently off topic? Do you call too many meetings? Too few? Spoken feedback is infinitely preferable, because then you have the chance to get clarification.

The other reason why feedback processes often flop is that organisations tend to focus on people's weaknesses and concentrate heavily on those areas rather than play to people's strengths and give lots of positive reinforcement. So people end up associating the word *feedback* with negatives. That is a completely backward approach, yet it happens every day. Weaknesses should be addressed, of course, but they should not become the primary focus. Think about a high-performing athlete. What do you think would happen if the athlete's coach hammered every day on the one aspect of his or her game that was weak?

So how do you get feedback that you haven't received before? Request it on a regular basis. Create informal opportunities and forums. I've known several leaders who routinely have lunch or breakfast with small groups of employees and encourage people to discuss issues. These smart leaders publicly praise and reward people who do speak up – especially about difficult topics. Commit to regular performance and progress reviews, so that everyone knows where they stand.

Stop and Reflect

Make personal disclosures about your own doubts and concerns, dreams and hopes.

If a business has a very closed culture, you may initially have to introduce non-face-to-face, anonymous ways of giving and receiving feedback. Request non-attributable agenda items to ensure important items get discussed but also that those who put them forward can remain anonymous.

In order to create an open and honest culture, nothing and no one – especially the leader – should be declared off limits. Too many businesses lose out when employees don't feel free to speak up. For example, your business team doesn't buy into your new marketing strategy, but no one on the team has the nerve to tell you. Or your top salesman, Fred, is belting down the booze at lunch with clients, but no one addresses his behaviour.

> **Leadership Note:** *Openness breeds openness.*

In mergers and acquisitions, cultural integrations are almost always very difficult, and that's because at the outset people aren't allowed to put concerns, doubts and fears on the table. Often, the CEO thinks only about the *business* reasons for a merger. The *people* part of the equation gets ignored, because the CEO doesn't want to discuss the negatives around the deal. Though it's counterintuitive, the smoothest M&A deals happen when people are allowed to voice their concerns in group settings. Even though there still may be some fear, employees in an open culture are much more likely to work through the obstacles and embrace change.

When I coach someone, I make an offer: 'I can open some secrets for you. What would you love to find out about you from the top people in your organisation (nonattributably) whom I'm interviewing in a feedback format? What views do you have about yourself and what do others think about you?'

Wake-up Call

Find a mirror and take a long hard look at yourself.

A marketing director in a retail business had sufficient self-awareness to know his natural style was command-and-control, and he'd experienced success with that style. The existing procedure for getting feedback in the company revolved around strengths, weaknesses, successes and disappointments. Once a year, everybody was asked to provide a summary based on those four categories.

While the answers to those questions were useful, they didn't help my client understand the downside to his leadership style. We came up with a set of questions to ask people. Feel free to use or adapt any or all of the following questions to help you to respond to the title of this chapter, 'Who are you, and who do others say you are?' You may be able to add to the list, depending on your own situation.

- How does it feel working around me?

- What do I do that helps your performance?

- What do I do that hinders your performance?

- What have you learned working with me and what would you like to learn?

- Do you experience me as supportive of your success? If so, how? If not, why?

- Do you believe I am committed to your career advancement? If so, how? If not, why?

- What do you want from me that you are not getting?

- What's one thing you'd like me to stop/start/continue doing that would help you be more effective?

We discovered two invaluable things he was completely unaware of.

First, people felt anxious working around him most of the time. His inconsistency in what he asked people to do provoked anxiety. His employees were never sure whether an agenda would stay or go. They couldn't discern whether something was truly important or whether the brouhaha would blow over next week. He was also inconsistent in how he responded to things. Some days he was relaxed; others, impatient. His staff were on edge, wondering, 'Which version are we going to see today?'

He also created tension by giving impossible deadlines and targets underlined by statements such as, 'Don't tell me it can't be done. Anything is possible.' He thought he was displaying a can-do attitude. He was horrified to find out how stressed he was making everyone around him.

Second, whereas he viewed himself as strongly committed to his employees' careers and advancement, his employees saw him as Machiavellian in his approach. While it was true that he thought about his employees' careers a lot and talked to them about it, his employees' view was, 'It's always about where *he* thinks we should go. It is his agenda, not ours.' When presented with that information, he admitted that he typically didn't elicit their responses and saw that the discussions were in reality more of a monologue.

He struck a deal with his team that whenever he was being inconsistent – in moods or requests – his employees would speak up to help him modify that behaviour. He also agreed to be open to their pushing back whenever he set a target or goal too high. To solve the other primary concern, we added a careers topic to the meeting agenda and included reminders to make the meeting a dialogue rather than a one-way conversation.

> **Leadership Note:** *Everything you do as a leader has meaning, import and impact.*

This fact is a double-edged sword: it's the big opportunity and, at the same time, the burden of leadership. Everything you do and say is significant, and everything about you can be potentially misinterpreted as it runs through the filters of the individuals with whom you come into contact. Perceptions are other people's realities.

For many years, the chairman and CEO of a large consumer-product company had always sponsored a racing car and maintained posh boxes at several important sporting events where clients were lavishly entertained. However, this company was experiencing dramatic cultural, structural and strategy changes in the business, so I was brought in to coach the current chairman/CEO on leading through the transition.

Two things had forced the enormous changes he was facing: some new antimonopoly legislation forced the company to sell off a piece of its business that had been significant; and new competition had entered the market with products that were considered exotic.

The company he led had been successful for many years. It was set in its ways with a predictable formula for success, but the competitive landscape had changed significantly.

As I helped him decide the moves to make for the future, we determined that the biggest challenge was leading the charge without de-motivating the workforce, many of whom came from families who had worked at the company for generations. He needed to bring the staff on board with his ideas to keep the company moving forward.

Stop and Reflect

Fully consider the consequences of any actions you are contemplating. Is it possible that your actions might bring a different reaction from the one you anticipate?

During the course of one of our coaching sessions, he announced that he'd decided to stop sponsoring the racing car. 'It's not a good use of our resources,' he said.

Intuition prompted me to observe, 'Sometimes a change you make in business can have a very different effect than the one you anticipate.'

He replied, 'I think my staff will see it positively and as appropriate to the new world order here.'

'Before you make a decision about the racing car, test the decision by telling your staff it's one of a number of changes being contemplated.'

When he solicited his staff's opinion, he got a strong reaction that he had not anticipated: the staff hated the idea. The employees saw the racing-car sponsorship as a symbol of success for the business rather than a waste of money. In fact, many expressed dismay at the thought, saying, 'If our boss is thinking of stopping the sponsorship, we must be in trouble.'

Wake-up Call

Set up the feedback process so that you get open, honest answers that are genuinely useful.

The 35-year-old CEO of a publishing company decided to step back from her hands-on leadership and encourage others to step up. So she began to delegate responsibilities, attend fewer meetings and increase the hours she worked from home. She used the time she saved for strategic planning.

I was asked to gauge the reaction of her direct reports, and in a series of interviews, I gathered their responses. She scanned ahead as I began to read her the report.

'What does this mean?' she interrupted me, pointing at the fifth bullet point on the page and looking stunned. 'They're questioning my credibility?'

'They interpret your stepping back from leadership as a loss of interest,' I told her. 'The team questions whether you should still lead.'

Furious now, she said, 'Well, if that's the way they feel, I don't want to stay here.'

Seldom had one of my clients reacted as strongly to feedback, and I was deeply concerned. The next day I followed up. 'I'm taking the week off. I'll decide whether to stay,' she said.

'Hold on. We both know you're committed to this business. You made a laudable effort to boost leadership, and your intentions were misconstrued. Did you ever tell them what you were doing and why?'

'No. It should be obvious.'

'You thought so, but they didn't get it. They misinterpreted.'

'After all I've done here, how could they possibly think I'm not committed?'

'Because they misunderstood. Go ahead and take some time to reflect. I'm available all next week if you need me.'

A week later she was calm and clear. 'I'm absolutely committed,' she told me. 'Now, help me fix this.'

'Get to your team,' I said. 'Talk straight, and tell them you simply stepped back too far. When they hear what you were trying to accomplish, they'll hear your passion for this business again.'

A year later, she asked me to conduct a similar feedback exercise, and this time all the marks were high. She said, 'When you told me last year that my credibility was in question, that was one of the best things that's happened. If I hadn't found out people thought I was losing interest, who knows where we'd be today? A long way downhill, I imagine.'

Leadership Note: *The only valuable feedback is honest feedback.*

I thanked her for telling me, because in her case, I wondered whether I should have softened the message – especially given her initial reaction. But I believe the only valuable feedback is honest feedback. And, as it turned out, sorting out the truth was a revitalising experience for her team, the business and her.

Wake-up Call

You will have to work hard to see and hear the truth.

A 60-year-old chief financial officer had worked in a consumer products company his entire career. He was married to his job, kept long hours and deftly managed a complex, difficult role. Excellent at communications, he had major responsibilities on the financial side of the company and in dealing with the financial and investment community. He was a tremendous asset to the business. And he believed that managers were omnipotent.

In contrast to his demanding style, the company was shifting to a much more open and informal culture. This radical transformation empowered people, and turnover in his department was rising rapidly because his harshness became even more glaringly obvious.

Omnipotence makes feedback pointless, but now for the first time he was required to hear it from his department. Why were his people leaving? What did they say about him?

His manager was confrontation-averse and didn't know how to deliver critical feedback. In turn, the executive was defensive and dismissive and made his disapproval of the process clear. So his manager asked me to intervene.

The executive refused to meet me.

I phoned one of his colleagues and asked if he could implore him to meet me just once. Eventually, his colleague succeeded. The executive would grant me exactly one hour, in a hotel lobby.

He sat bolt upright and addressed me formally as 'Mr Alexander'. Everything about him seemed to highlight the rigidity of his demeanour. For 50 minutes he hardly spoke. At that point I gambled.

'At the risk of never seeing you again, I need to speak frankly,' I said. 'I've observed you today and read the reports from your department. I'm absolutely certain that, for all your working life, you've been dedicated to this company. You have remarkably high standards and you manage your part of the business exceedingly well. And now you see the business changing. You don't approve, and you aren't interested in adapting. Plus, thirty years into your career, you've been given critical feedback that must have hurt you deeply.'

He rose abruptly from his seat, shook my hand, and said, 'Mr Alexander, I know you wish to be helpful, but I don't want to pursue this with you.' He turned on his heels and left. I assumed that was the end of it, but the following day his secretary called to schedule another meeting in the hotel lobby.

He materialised on the dot and strode across the lobby. 'Thank you for arranging to see me today,' he said. 'I must tell you, Mr Alexander, that your summary of my experience was quite accurate.'

He kept his emotions carefully in check, but I could see that he was shaken. We began to discuss his options. He allowed for only two: learn the new management style, and stay until he reached the company's retirement age of 65, or retire early.

He acknowledged that five more years in the new culture would be torturous. He also acknowledged that his loyalty to the company made it nearly impossible to consider early retirement. Early retirement presented financial challenges as well. But, if the company handled those challenges, would he consider retiring now? His loyalty to the company was fading as we talked about how much he would have to change to stay, and how it felt as if the company had moved on without him.

We came up with a circumstance under which he'd be comfortable leaving. 'Talk to your boss to see if that's possible,' I said.

He dug in his heels. I offered to go to his boss on his behalf, and he agreed.

I carried his decision to the CEO. 'No way,' said the CEO. 'He has to listen to the feedback, change his management style and work out his five years.'

'He's already given you thirty years of exemplary performance,' I said. 'The only reason he's being discussed now is that the rules of the business have changed. He's still every bit as devoted and competent as he ever was. Why not make this a win–win? Celebrate his years of achievement and let him leave with dignity.'

The package was bigger than he expected.

A year later, I received an email: 'Graham, I believe this has been the happiest year of my life. I see now I should have left years earlier. I am travelling to places I always dreamed of seeing. I've learned to play the guitar. And I wish you could see my new red convertible Mini Cooper!'

A convertible?

Million-dollar Question

Where are you out of touch with reality?

Many leaders are off the mark in several critical areas. A classic example that I've encountered over and over again is that most leaders don't actually know where they spend their time. I often ask people I'm coaching to break down their role into a number of headings and estimate the percentage of time or hours per week they spend under each heading. Then we do an analysis of where they *think* their time and energy is being spent and where it is *actually* being spent. In almost every case, there are wide discrepancies. On occasions, we've discovered an hour and a half a day clearing emails – most of which are irrelevant.

Another example: the CEO prides himself on being known by the employees and being a good communicator in terms of where the business is going. Then I get into the lift with him and, clearly, the employees don't know who he is – much less what his vision for the company is.

Or the CEO tells me she spends time with her key people, but her key people feel she is so busy that they can't ask for the time they need or want. Another common blind spot: the CEO thinks he is operating at a high level and not in detail. But his people say he is persistently overinvolved in the details of the business.

Wake-up Call

How you see yourself is irrelevant.

The just-promoted marketing director of one of the largest companies in Australia asked me how he could turn himself into a great leader and his team into high-performance thoroughbreds.

'What's your background?' I asked.

'Pubs, mostly. Football, parties, and bad jokes.'

He wasn't entirely kidding. That's the blue-collar culture of his industry.

To come up through those ranks into senior leadership presented challenges. More than most do when they switch from worker to manager to leader, he would have to change. I suggested we draw an old boy/new man matrix on a chart and begin to separate pub antics from boardroom conduct. He could change his behaviours accordingly.

It went swimmingly until he came across activities he was reluctant to forgo. He didn't want to give up evenings at the pub with his former peer group, for example. And he wasn't pleased to ponder the end of laddishness – the bawdy jokes and late-night pints.

Could he be a leader without relinquishing those satisfying peer connections?

Million-dollar Question

Do you know exactly what everyone expects of you as a leader?

And, since he had achieved success while being 'one of the boys', why change now? A member of the gang can become its leader easily enough. But what happens when he moves on to a top executive spot?

We talked through those questions, and he began to make slight shifts in his behaviour as he groomed himself for a spot on the board. I could see, however, that he was especially distressed about giving up the frequent visits to the pub. 'I know it seems trivial, but I'm worried that the guys will think I'm acting above my station,' he said.

'Is there somebody in the group that you can speak to confidentially about your dilemma?' I asked.

He went to one of his friends, who advised, 'Don't worry. For a week or two, don't come. Everybody knows you're busy in your new role. Gradually, the expectation that you should be there will fade away. It'll happen naturally.'

> **Leadership Note:** *Seek wise counsel from somebody in the middle of the issue.*

First, he replaced the social interaction at the pub with regular, slightly more formal team dinners. Second, the risqué jokes retreated into history. Third, he added a column called 'MAN OF TOMORROW' to his old boy/new man matrix and began to picture a seat on the board. 'Imagine yourself as an elder statesman,' I suggested.

Next, in meetings with his staff, he painted the big picture, positioning topics within the wider view of the company's goals and resources and helping people see how they fitted in. Finally, he asked me how he came across, and I said, 'Energetic, ambitious and capable, but frankly, from your shoes to your haircut, you come across like a teenager in a grown-up's body. When your capability is out of sync with your appearance, you have to work harder with people to gain their confidence.'

He bought a couple of Italian suits and paid more than he thought prudent for a haircut. And, as he zeroed in on the details, he grew into a remarkable executive.

Wake-up Call

Don't demand of your people what you're not demanding of yourself.

A CEO new in his role at the helm of a large US company hired me. The company held several key values as important, and he wanted to get off on the right foot, so he called me in to help him align with those key values.

Early on, I identified an area of concern: he smoked in his office. Even after a building-wide ban was introduced as part of the company's commitment to ensuring a pleasant working environment, he routinely lit up. 'It's my call,' he said, somewhat defensively when I asked about his habit. 'And probably 99 per cent of the staff don't see me.'

'Isn't it interesting that you find no credibility issues here with your role as CEO, your behaviour and the building policy? Tell me, how many people in this building know that you smoke in your office?'

'Probably all of them.' He smiled and said, 'I suppose I've given them something to gossip about. Shooting myself in the foot, aren't I?'

He stopped smoking in his office, acknowledged to his staff that he'd been out of line, and won some respect.

Then, during a round of company-wide cost cutting, he told me that he'd decided against purchasing a corporate jet. The company was in a cost-cutting mode, and he never dreamed that the board would think it a wise expenditure. 'But you travel all the time for business, and I'm not sure that's the wisest decision,' I said, urging him to take the issue before the board.

To his surprise, the board approved the expenditure. It was eager to support an executive who served as an ambassador for the business.

Million-dollar Question

What's the one missing piece in your puzzle – and does it say something about who you are?

One area that clients often have a great deal of uncertainty around is the reality of their financial picture. That may sound surprising. Over and over again, however, I've seen that many high-performing leaders may be great when it comes to dealing with the finances of their companies, but their own finances often get short shrift. Although they are good at making a lot of money – a safe assumption since a single coaching session with me costs a not inconsiderable amount of money – many are miserably ineffective at managing it.

I think this phenomenon occurs for two reasons. First, top leaders are so busy that taking the time to focus on their own finances seems overwhelming, so personal financial management gets shoved to the bottom of the priority list. Besides, for many, money is a by-product of the game they enjoy, which is business. Money merely represents the chips that allow them to stay in the game. Second, some of the best performers in the world come from modest means, and their childhood experiences – sometimes painful – have shaped their views of money. These clients often have a skewed view of their financial situations. Either way, the subject of money is sensitive for most people.

I routinely try to get my clients to think about their attitudes regarding money in relation to their self-awareness, because how you handle and view your money is another reflection of how you view yourself. Of course, if your perception of your monetary situation is off, that naturally throws other areas of your life out of kilter, too.

Although I don't like to generalise – because everyone is unique – over the years I've often found that top-performing women tend to underestimate their financial success while men are often overly optimistic.

The 35-year-old marketing director of a major leisure company came to me as a referral client. Initially, our agenda was to work on her time-management skills and personal organisation. As I got to know her, I saw that, although she earned a generous salary, she spent little of her money. She had grown up in a poor family. In the course of one session, we were looking at her calendar, and I asked, 'How much holiday do you take annually?'

She replied, 'I always take five weeks.'

'What do you do with your holiday time?'

'Oh, I never really go away. I stick around home.'

Something about the wistful way she said it caught me. 'Don't you enjoy travelling? After all, you're young and single. I would have thought you'd want to see some of the world.'

'I love travelling, but I'm concerned about spending more than I should. I don't want to run out of money.'

'Would it be useful to do a financial analysis to see where you stand?'

Leadership Note: *Fear of the unknown is a heavy weight.*

She agreed to my suggestion. If she was worrying needlessly, she needed to be free of that millstone around her neck. But, if the financial checkup showed cause for concern, she would at least have that information to begin to take steps to rectify the situation.

Once we'd done an analysis of her financial status, she was flabbergasted to learn that she had amassed more than a million pounds. That knowledge gave her the comfort level she needed to make some different choices. She'd been holding back based on a feeling rather than a reality. Now she could do what she loved to do instead of living in false dread over impending financial disaster that wasn't even close to happening.

She bought herself a nice car, and during our next session I asked her where her dream holiday would be. 'The Maldives in the Indian Ocean,' she said.

Then I asked her another question, 'Why don't you book yourself a trip?'

Stop and Reflect

What are you lying about to yourself or others? List what you haven't said or have fudged about to your colleagues. Perhaps you still view yourself as an athlete when you haven't done anything physical in years. Maybe you see yourself as an encouraging person while your colleagues would say that they cannot remember the last time you uttered a compliment.

We have looked at several roads to self-examination in this chapter. We have had the benefit of some case histories and there are a number of questions you can ask yourself on this voyage of self-discovery. Do you know who you are? Is that the same person as the person others see you as? Have you been surprised that the two may not always have been the same person? Try to discover things about yourself that could make that vital difference.

Executive Summary

Million-dollar Questions

- What knowledge about yourself are you missing that could make a significant difference in your life and/or your company's performance?

- What is the effect of your leadership style? Does it state who you are – both to you and to others? And does it tell you how others see you?

- Where are you out of touch with reality?

- Do you know exactly what everyone expects of you as a leader?

- What's the one missing piece in your puzzle – and does it say something about who you are?

Stop and Reflect

- Consider the type of person you are. List key questions about yourself and try to answer them. Then get honest answers from those around you – your life partner, your personal assistant, a trusted adviser, and select employees in the company. How do their answers compare with yours?

- Write down three roles you've had in your career where you've been most satisfied. Does your current role look like any of the three that you wrote down?

- Make personal disclosures about your own doubts and concerns, dreams and hopes.

- Fully consider the consequences of any actions you are contemplating. Is it possible that your actions might bring a different reaction from the one you anticipate?

- What are you lying about to yourself or others? List what you haven't said or have fudged about to your colleagues.

Wake-up Calls

- Task, task, task. Do, do, do. No review. If this sounds like the rhythm of your day, this chapter has been for you, and you may gain by reading it again.

- Don't let too much depend on you.

- Take time to be clear about your wants, your needs, your strengths, your weaknesses.

- When your life is driven by 'shoulds' and 'must-dos' you are in danger of losing your genuine self.

- Find a mirror and take a long hard look at yourself.

- Set up the feedback process so that you get open, honest answers that are genuinely useful.

- You will have to work hard to see and hear the truth.

- How you see yourself is irrelevant.

- Don't demand of your people what you're not demanding of yourself.

Leadership Notes

- Know thyself – and let thyself be known.

- Be more true to yourself in your business. Don't try to be something you are not.

- Remember that openness breeds openness.

- Everything you do as a leader has meaning, import and impact.

- The only valuable feedback is honest feedback.

- Seek wise counsel from somebody in the middle of the issue.

- Fear of the unknown is a heavy weight.

What's the point for you and your people?

WHEN A REPORTER ASKED a cleaner at NASA what his job was, the man famously answered, 'I'm helping put a man on the moon.' He was connected and inspired by the mission.

People need meaning in their lives. You do, and your staff do. Yet most company mission statements have little or no motivational impact. Most that I see can be boiled down to a single, uninspiring phrase: 'increasing shareholder value'. Does that get you up in the morning? I doubt it. And you can bet that no one else on your team finds it motivating.

The highest-performing leaders create enlivening stories and myths that communicate the mission, vision, values and goals of the company. They never stop communicating those. They want everyone to have a common view. These leaders know it's impossible to overcommunicate about the vision and mission and where the company is going. They talk about them until those key thoughts become ingrained in their employees' thoughts.

Have you as a leader created some way of talking about the business that inspires your people? On a peak-performing team, every member plays his or her part and contributes. That only happens when everyone understands the ultimate goal or mission.

Recently, I was walking up the Jetway to board a transatlantic flight when the British Airways gate agent came running. 'Mr Alexander, I noticed that there are two infants seated near you,' he said, out of breath from sprinting after me. 'I'd like to move you to an area where you'll find three empty seats. I think you'd be far more comfortable there. Would you mind coming back with me to the gate, so I can make the change?' Of course, I was all too happy to accompany him back to the gate. He demonstrated that he was in tune with his company's mission: to give travellers 'the kind of travel experience you'd love to have'.

My mission statement is 'having a life- and performance-enhancing impact in the world of work'. _That's much more inspiring than saying, 'I am a consultant specialising in leadership and coaching'. The former is a powerful statement that conveys that I care about you in my business.

Stop and Reflect

Ask yourself, what's the point? Human nature causes each of us to seek a purpose. Working to put your purpose in life on paper will yield clarity.

Write a mission statement for you and your business that connects the work to making the world a better place. Another way to think about it is to ask, what would you want on your gravestone?

When you step up to a bigger role, it's easy to lose sight of your mission. That almost happened to one executive, a strong and successful CEO of a design firm. He had established himself as a visionary in the field of home furnishings and was recruited to be the design director for an even bigger, multi-product-stream retailer. Once there, however, he felt out of place. It was a much more bureaucratic, unaccountable and nonreactive culture, and he struggled to get anything done. He began to think he was losing his creativity and design sense. That was when we met.

I conducted a set of interviews for the chief executive, who was also relatively new to the company, to help her understand his challenges. In the course of our work together, she introduced me to the new design director.

He asked me what I did. 'I coach senior executives,' I said. He told me about himself and about the difficulties he faced – especially his feeling that he was losing his creative flair. I learned he had a coach who was helping him with a long-term career plan, so I didn't see him as a coaching prospect. But I offered him a no-obligation exploratory meeting and suggested that we might look at how he could retain his creative spark and not be sapped by the company's complex and slow-response culture.

Million-dollar Question

What is your underlying purpose in life?

I didn't hear from him for quite a long time. Then one day he called and said he'd like to take the next step. We met, and I asked him to define in a personal mission statement what his professional life was fundamentally about – what drove him in his work.

I often ask people to identify their underlying purposes and driving forces. I tell them to look back through their lives to the times when they felt most successful and satisfied, and write descriptions of those experiences. Now, what typically happens is that themes surface, and people discover what they're about, what turns them on, why they're here – in other words, what the point is. When the themes resonate with truth and depth, people will see that they've actually written their personal mission statements.

Stop and Reflect

Pick out six to eight times in your life when you felt successful and satisfied. Write down these projects and incidents. Describe in detail the qualities of these experiences. Look for the commonalities. If you are struggling to define your mission in life, this simple exercise will often lead you down the right path.

The above exercise should give you the beginning of your personal mission statement. It is not just a set of clever words: your mission statement must resonate with and express your passion.

The design director wrote, 'Giving people more beauty than they thought possible' – a statement that certainly resonated with him and reflected his passion for bringing wonderful, beautiful home furnishings into mundane, everyday life.

'Do you see that as a phrase that will infect the people in the business and you with excitement?' I asked. The challenge was to find something consistent with his purpose and capture it in a phrase that could affect people at work around him and inspire them to get things done. We agreed, however, that his phrase was a little abstract and could potentially confuse or turn people off.

His next attempt was 'bringing aspirational quality to all'. Again, it was consistent with his purpose, but more fine-tuning was needed. That was when he wrote, 'Making dreams for the home come true'. Those words captured something special – how he helps people build their enjoyment of their surroundings by making their dream houses come true. Identifying this purpose statement helped him recover his creativity and inspiration. And, when he returned to his workplace, the change was both evident and infectious. Inspired again, he motivated and energised others.

Million-dollar Question

If you were an employee in your organisation, what would you want from you as a boss? Put yourself in the shoes of those whom you lead.

When the CEO of a manufacturing business retired, he left something special behind for his successor: gloom. His legacy of ruthless cost cutting, his get-tough approach to people and his frequent messages of doom over the years – all of which he intended as wake-up calls – had only succeeded in rendering his employees fearful, depressed and unmotivated.

The new CEO arrived just as the switch to the euro was opening up trade opportunities for the company, providing not only terrific new opportunities for growth, but fresh competition from other European companies, too. It should have been a great time for the business to rise to the challenges; unfortunately, the employees' lack of motivation left the place at a standstill. What the CEO needed was a reversal in attitude – and fast!

To refocus their vision, I helped the CEO and his top team craft a new mission statement that captured the spirit of their previous successes and recalled their company's glory days – even touching their strong sense of national pride. Rich with connotations, good memories and hopes, the statement became the rallying call – from top management right down to the factory floor – that started the business on the path to a turnaround.

Wake-up Call

Beware the vague mission statement.

As the retailer slipped from first place to third, the CEO called for a redefinition of the company's mission.

'We'll reclaim number one!' he pledged.

As the retailer slipped towards fourth place, the old CEO was pushed out, and the new CEO questioned the mission.

'Getting back to the top – that's more like an outcome than a purpose,' he said. 'At the storefront level, it doesn't tell people what to do. Let's find a purpose that motivates.'

So, from head office to back office and all the stores in between, he had managers run information-gathering sessions. There was only one question: 'What's the purpose of this business?'

The answers were surprisingly similar: 'We make the right products readily available to our customers at the right price.' Eventually, we drafted a mission statement that focused on customer satisfaction instead of market position, and the revised mission statement helped breathe new life into the company.

Wake-up Call

Don't take yourself too seriously.

Perfectionism can drive success – if it doesn't kill you first. When a communications director for a large insurance company struggled with turmoil at work and at home, his pursuit of perfection had him headed in the wrong direction.

At work, the combined effects of shifting market conditions, the exploration of new sales channels, and changes in regulations put the company under stress. That meant the communications director was on the line – answering to shareholders, employees and press. It also meant that his work represented a ceaseless onslaught of needs with little satisfaction in return.

Meanwhile, his wife had grown resentful of his attentiveness to workplace demands, which often came at the expense of quality time with her and their three sons. He experienced his wife's frustration as a loss of support that placed even greater demands on his energy and time.

Determined always to give 100 per cent of himself to everything and unable to fail, he was floundering in a torrent of demands and losing focus on what mattered. It seemed only a matter of time before irreparable damage occurred in his health, family life or career.

Stop and Reflect _____

Post reminders of your mission and mottos that help you achieve your goals.

I encouraged him to write a motto that would help him to step back from the tumult, an idea he could use to remind himself not to become completely lost in the process. He came up with two:

- Play as if your life depends on it – and always remember that it doesn't.

- Fight only the battles you can win.

Naturally, being the perfectionist he was, he posted these two mottos everywhere – on his computer's screensaver, on his bathroom mirror, on a sign at his desk, in his wallet. And it worked. Not long afterwards, he reported walking through the reception area and becoming instantly incensed that someone had left some rubbish on a table. As he fought off his fierce impulse to bang out a critical email, he reminded himself that the reception area wasn't his responsibility. And dealing with somebody else's responsibility, given his difficulties, was a waste of his time.

That was exactly when his will to survive won out over his perfectionism, a victory that continued to serve him well throughout that stressful period with his company.

Stop and Reflect

Imagine that you are sitting by a pool in two years' time, sipping a tropical drink and saying how fantastic the last two years have been. What happened in those last two years?

Wake-up Call

Go on a treasure hunt to find the key to unlocking your mission.

Some of us have more difficulty figuring out what our mission is than others. If you're left-brained – like many of my clients – this chapter may seem too ethereal to you. Keep reading.

Furthermore, even if you have written a mission statement for your company, that doesn't mean that your people connect with it in a meaningful way. Many companies and teams with whom I've worked find it useful to take the existing mission statement and examine it as a group to see how it translates compared with what the group believe it should be.

When I'm working with a group on this topic, I typically insist that we meet at an offsite spot. A change of scenery helps people think differently. Then we embark on some exercises.

First, take a large piece of paper (a flipchart works well). Give everyone crayons, pens, markers or chalk. Ask the participants to draw on one half of the paper a picture of how the business is now, and then on the other half to draw a picture of how the business would be if it were a success. Tell them they are not being judged on artistic merit!

Each team member pins his or her picture on the wall. Then we walk the group from picture to picture and have the 'artist' in each case talk about what it means personally to him or her. The purpose is to get everyone thinking in a much more right-brained manner – meaning emotionally and creatively – rather than left-brained, which governs rationality and strategic thinking. As a group, discuss common themes in the desired future state. Out of these common aspirations for the business, you can start to structure a mission statement and a set of values for the business.

Another good exercise is to have team members write the announcement of their retirement and describe what had been achieved in that business while they were there. Or have members write what they would want written on their gravestones. These exercises get all parties to think longer-term about what they would like to contribute or create in the organisation.

My favourite exercise always brings surprises. I ask everyone to come to the meeting with two items – one that represents their work life in some meaningful way and one that holds some importance in their personal life. The results are always completely unpredictable. One person might bring a guitar and a business letter from a customer saying how much he or she appreciated the company and the service the person gave. Another might bring a favourite family photo and an email from a colleague thanking the individual for his or her leadership. Then we talk about what they brought and why it holds meaning for them.

In another version of this same exercise, I ask people to bring one personal item and *two* for the business – one that relates inside the company, its people and culture that has real meaning for them, and one that relates to customers and clients outside of the company.

These exercises enable us to see what common themes emerge and use them to draft a mission/purpose statement. It's a powerful way of getting people to talk from their hearts rather than from the left-brained rationality generally exhibited in a work setting.

Stop and Reflect

Identify a personal experience that is relevant to the challenges your people are currently facing.

A CEO with a financial background – a real numbers man – was known as blind to the people side of business. Everybody thought he ran the business as a mathematical exercise in which there was no room for humanity.

At the annual executive retreat, he was full of surprises. First, he brought a book on multiple sclerosis. He revealed that his wife had MS, and he talked about the incredible challenges of caring for a person whose health was so tenuous. He described his nonworking time and how engaged he was in creating a wonderful life for his family and taking full advantage of the times when his wife's illness went into remission.

He also revealed that they were going through another re-adjustment stage, since her MS had recently reared its ugly head and was wreaking havoc in their lives.

Since no one in the group knew about his wife's illness, the revelation immediately shifted their perceptions of this 'numbers man'. And that was just the beginning, because the second thing he brought was a ring binder full of personal notes, emails and several exit interviews – a big file filled with positive messages from people about how the business had helped their careers. He said, 'Over and above the fact that I want ours to be a profitable business with increasing shareholder value, what counts for me is that our people find their careers here rewarding and fulfilling.'

He pointed to the book and said, 'I save all this, because these notes remind me that our employees' experiences here make their lives better.'

This man had never talked about his personal life at work, and so people were surprised to learn of his tender side, and his employees were astounded that he obviously had given so much thought and cared so deeply about the people side of the business.

These revelations transformed their picture of him and sparked a discussion about reshaping the company's mission to reflect the important role of people in the business.

Wake-up Call

Show your own emotions – and you'll touch theirs.

Many high level leaders somehow believe that revealing much about their personalities or personal lives will dilute ther position of authority. However, over and over again, I've noted that the most effective leaders are those who are willing to show their humanity and reveal their true selves to their employees.

I recall the CEO whose self-presentation was always buttoned down, completely professional and appropriate, very conservative. She never joked, although she was pleasant enough. In every circumstance and with all her people she made it absolutely clear she meant business.

What no one knew was that her passion was fast cars. She brought a British Grand Prix Formula One pit lane pass to the session. Her colleagues were stunned – and at least a little bit relieved to learn that their strictly businesslike CEO also had a decidedly unbusinesslike side. Businesspeople are real people. It helps to rediscover that.

> **Leadership Note:** *Constantly remind yourself that everyone is unique.*

Over a quarter of a century of coaching, several inner drivers have emerged in the people with whom I've worked. Some are motivated by status, power, influence and money. Some are out to prove themselves to others.

Innovators strive to do something that's never been done before – to turn an idea or insight into a commercial reality. Some people love turning companies around.

Still others are driven to produce excellence, and most businesses aren't excellent. Many leaders simply enjoy the intellectual challenge of business. The socially conscious businessperson wants to affect human beings' lives – both customers' and staff's – in a positive way. This person typically has a crystal clear and powerful sense of purpose and is able to help others in the company embrace that vision.

I've had some clients who were drawn to companies that have such strong brands and histories that they are established as pillars in the economy and communities in which they operate. They see the companies as a part of their heritage and want to have a hand in perpetuating that.

Finally, some are driven by dangerous revenge. I've worked with a few people who had been passed over for a top job, and it becomes a significant driver to kill the competitive company that didn't give them the top job. That's dangerous because you can become too narrowly focused, and a personal mission with a negative force is virtually impossible to rally others around.

Stop and Reflect

Gather your top team around a table and have the leader name the chief driver for each person there. Ideally, the individuals' drivers should somehow connect to the company's mission.

I knew a brilliant product innovator. He suffered from dyslexia, had been a poor student and was driven to prove to his former teachers that he could make something of himself. His technical and wholly innovative approaches led him to become a stellar performer, but what he did was so arcane that the people who worked with him struggled to understand it. I explained to him that getting his employees to rally around his personal mission of innovating in this difficult field simply wouldn't work.

His success was demonstrated by a huge income. But at home the evidence of his success was scattered willy-nilly – unbanked cheques, unpaid bills and troves of cash simply littered his house. To address the disorganisation that was at odds with his career, I challenged him to collect all the cheques and cash lying around his house before the next coaching session.

He found about £300,000! Money simply wasn't a driver for him. What continued to matter the most in his life was his work, not the monetary reward that came with his success.

Million-dollar Question

If you were a member of your team or an employee in your business, what would make your work life gratifying?

How successful you and your organisation are at accomplishing your mission is directly related to how the people with whom you work are feeling. Too many leaders mouth the words 'people are our greatest assets.' But they don't put themselves in others' shoes or take the time to communicate fully with employees.

We make all kinds of assumptions about what the people who are putting in eight to twelve hours a day on the job are thinking, but we don't ask them directly. You don't have to be a psychologist to figure out what makes people happy. Most people work hard but aren't very happy. The desire to be inspired, motivated, interested and appreciated is universal. Rare is the leader, however, who consciously thinks about how to draw the best out of people, despite mission statements that pay lip service to the idea. What's the point for your people if you can't help them to operate at their full potential? What's the point for you?

Stop and Reflect

Think about your work environment for a moment. What words come to mind? 'Fun', 'freedom', 'creative', 'energised'? Or 'bureaucratic', 'stifling', 'drab', 'pressured'?

One way to get the best out of people is to show appreciation. A lot of leaders don't think to thank people for the jobs they do. That's just as sad as having a partner at home who is never appreciated. We all crave thank-yous, appreciation and recognition. Walk around almost any office, and I guarantee you'll spot handwritten thank-you notes posted. Ignore the simple things such as knowing people's names and asking about their kids, and your organisation will suffer. Don't underestimate the relationship between a motivated workforce and good business performance.

An athlete breaks down very quickly if the sport is no longer fun. It's the same with your people. The workplace should provide a quality experience – not just a paycheque. *That's* the point.

Wake-up Call

Don't confuse making money with your purpose.

A multimillionaire who, before the age of 40, took her company public, who owned half a dozen exotic cars, including a Ferrari, three planes and several homes, was driven by the memory of being raised in poverty. Now, she supported her parents, her siblings and half a dozen family members. She gave generous bonuses.

She was also a workaholic whose relentless drive for more, more, more had already broken up two marriages and now threatened her third.

'What's next?' I asked her. 'When do you think you'll have enough?'

'I don't know. It's always been about more,' she said. 'People say I'm pretty much just in it for the money. But I enjoy all the toys. I don't see a problem.'

I wasn't trying to prove to her that her aspiration for wealth was wrong. Rather I was simply trying to get her to question whether it should continue as the sole driver in this new phase for the company and in her life.

'And *are* you just in it for the money?' I asked her. 'How do you want the last chapter of your life to read? What was the point of your life? If the end of your life was today, would you tell me it was about making money and supporting others?' Our conversation dragged on for weeks while she tried out one idea after another.

> ### Stop and Reflect
> Recognise the transformational points in your life and re-evaluate your mission and vision on a regular basis.

'Here's my last chapter,' she announced one day. 'My life was about an enormously successful business that also did good things in an innovative way and made a difference. You once asked me how much is enough. Well, it's when I can see that we've made a difference.'

The difference she had in mind was to transform her chain of continuing-education and tutoring programme centres into highly innovative ones that would address the issue of learning differences. She became personally involved. She joined the boards of several universities and formed student focus groups to explore learning differences and how to help children who had difficulty with the standard ways of teaching in traditional schools. She videotaped students talking about what it's like to struggle in class and what it's like to know you think differently from those around you. She asked her employees, 'How would you feel if this child were yours?'

The more involved she became, the more passionate she was about this niche and the more excited her people became about the new mission. They were no longer just making money with learning centres. They were helping youngsters who were not being served by the current educational system. The entrepreneur had successfully rallied them to a cause.

Million-dollar Question

What do your staff want?

The innovative learning projects brought new passion to the business. She and the company took pride in the centres that helped kids who were bright but bored, or underserved in traditional educational settings. She could see that her company made a difference, and she found it profoundly satisfying. She'd met both her new aspirations: creating a business that had never been done before, and making learning fun for youngsters whose needs had previously been neglected.

She also kept her Ferrari.

Stop and Reflect

Never allow yourself to be put in a box and don't put others there.

You need to get in touch with what turns your staff on. Everyone is different and has different needs. What gets one person excited may leave another flat. A good leader figures out how to tap into the common mission that will become a rallying cry for the company. That is why it is so important to know what the point is for you – *and* for your people.

Wake-up Call

**Figure out what the drivers are
for the key players around you.**

List what you expect each of your colleagues would answer to the question: What turns you on about this company/department/ your job?

Leadership Note: *Make life a game worth playing.*

Executive Summary

Million-dollar Questions

- What is your underlying purpose in life?

- If you were an employee in your organisation, what would you want from the person you are now?

- If you were a member of your team or an employee in your business, what would make your work life gratifying?

- What do your staff want?

Stop and Reflect

- Ask yourself, What's the point?

- Pick out six to eight times in your life when you felt successful and satisfied. Write down these projects and incidents. Describe in detail the qualities of these experiences. Look for the commonalities.

- Post reminders of your mission and mottos that help you achieve your goals.

- Imagine that you are sitting by a pool in two years' time, sipping a tropical drink and saying how fantastic the last two years have been. What happened in those last two years?

- Identify a personal experience that is relevant to the challenges your people are currently facing.

- Gather your top team around a table and have the leader name the chief driver for each person there. Ideally, the individuals' drivers should somehow connect to the company's mission.

- Think about your work environment for a moment. What words come to mind? 'Fun', 'freedom', 'creative', 'energised'? Or 'bureaucratic', 'stifling', 'drab', 'pressured'?

- Recognise the transformational points in your life and re-evaluate your mission and vision on a regular basis.

- Never allow yourself to be put in a box and don't put others there.

Wake-up Calls

- Beware the vague mission statement.

- Don't take yourself too seriously.

- Go on a treasure hunt to find the key to unlocking your mission.

- Show your own emotions – and you'll touch those of your people.

- Making money is an outcome, not a purpose.

- Figure out what the drivers are for the key players around you.

Leadership Notes

- Constantly remind yourself that everyone is unique.

- Make life a game worth playing.

What Would Happen If You Did Less?

I SEE MADNESS AT THE TOP of the ladder to success.

Leaders are losing focus on the key aspects of the business for one simple reason: they attempt to accomplish too much on a daily basis. One CEO I coached had more than 600 items on his to-do list. When I asked another CEO to walk me through his to-do list, he scarcely paused for a breath as he rattled off a daunting 120 items from memory. No wonder he never bothered to write it all down. I was overwhelmed – and it wasn't even my list.

Realistically, there is never going to be a time when nothing is on your plate. Leaders constantly see new things to fix or act upon. Moreover, senior executives who have forged successful careers by getting things done often respond to pressure by saddling themselves with exhaustive – and exhausting – action lists.

With downsizing, economic uncertainty and ruthless cost cutting, everyone has been forced to do more with fewer people and resources. Add the tyranny of the demand constantly to increase shareholder value in publicly held companies, and you have almost unattainable expectations on top leaders.

When you are scrutinised from all directions, the temptation to keep busy and to be seen as constantly in motion can be intense. The overwhelming majority of top leaders with whom I've worked had bought into the popular notion that part of their job was to be a role model and hence to work long, hard hours. The problem comes when working hard becomes a value in and of itself. Many people confuse working long, hard hours with achieving results.

During our one-on-one sessions, almost all leaders agree that they believe in a sensible work–life balance. Indeed, they crave it and often name more balance in their lives as one of their chief aims. However, most leaders are driven by the fear – in some cases, verging on a pathological level – of what would happen if they did less.

'Cut back on my hours and the amount of work I do each day?' Some CEOs visibly recoil when I suggest such a thing.

Ironically, the most powerful people – who in theory should wield more control over their lives – often view themselves as chained to their horrific work schedules by virtue of their position in the organisations they lead. Feeling powerless is a scary state of being for people who are called upon to be almost superhuman in their performance.

One of the most common traps many senior executives allow themselves to fall into is working at too low a level. Worried that they'll miss something important, they end up consumed by details. They fail to delegate items that they should. The result? They get bogged down in the minutiae of running the business, rather than concentrating on the actions that would further their business success and bring greater satisfaction and achievement.

You must focus your attention, time and energy on the key things that will move your business forward. For example, a CEO is predominantly paid for leading in four key areas:

- formulating strategy and vision;

- dealing with customers/clients;

- representing the company to the external world of analysts, press, and shareholders; and

- inspiring the people inside their own organisation to be excellent.

Figure out the handful of areas – no more than a dozen – for which you are responsible as a leader, and use them as a filter. Then go through your to-do list or action plan. See which items fall into one of those categories and which fall outside the filter – and thus deserve to be removed from your agenda. If you're like most leaders, doing this will probably narrow your to-do list considerably.

Now, which one item could you do today that would add the biggest value to the business? Another way to identify the one thing that would make the biggest difference is to think about your annual objectives or goals.

Million-dollar Question

If you did one thing that would move you towards accomplishing your most important goal, what would it be?

When I ask that million-dollar question in a session, the person usually produces an answer in lightning speed. It could be as simple as one phone call. Whatever it is, it's always at the top of your mind. Now we just have to make sure that whatever just popped into your head is at the top of your to-do list today.

Another important question is this: is your agenda doable? More than 75 per cent of the CEOs I have coached have answered a resounding no to that question, and more than 95 per cent have found their agendas undoable if they seriously want to accomplish what they want in life. For example, many CEOs say they want to spend more time with their children and spouses, they want to get fit, they want to see friends more often or they want to devote time to a hobby.

Stop and Reflect

Begin the process of trimming that to-do list by accepting that you are not superhuman.

List what has been added to your agenda over the recent past and what has been removed. Quantify whether it has increased, decreased, or stayed the same. Is the equation a net plus or minus? Have you filled your agenda with too many meetings, with meetings that go on too long, with too many operational items that should have been delegated to other people?

Seeing ourselves clearly can be difficult. I find that the leader's personal assistant (PA) often has a really good idea of how the leader is using his or her time. Once I get the OK from the leader, I schedule a three-way meeting to bring the PA in as a partner to protect the leader's time. The PAs love it.

I encourage executives to ask their PAs questions such as:

- Where do you see that my time is leaking away?

- Where am I getting involved in things that are not the best use of me?

- How can you and I work most effectively together?

> **Leadership Note:** *Businesses and leaders reduce their own effectiveness when they attempt too much.*

Rarely will a PA volunteer that information, but most have an opinion. These are simple questions, but, in the heat of the battle, people don't always ask them. Seek input from those who work closest with you and enlist their help in guarding your most precious resource: your time.

Wake-up Call

**Do not add to your agenda
unless you drop something else.**

Another trap I find within organisations is that the number of new initiatives on the business plan is at overload capacity. Too many projects are going on at one time.

When a new CEO came into a major company, he proceeded to make sweeping changes. He made an acquisition and replaced members of the top team. A new global IT system transformed the supply chain from factory to consumer.

In addition to those sweeping changes, the new CEO implemented a global restructuring to turn the business from a classical hierarchical structure to a matrix structure. He also instituted a major culture-change programme across the business aimed at making the company much more innovative. The company was involved in a push to segment its customers and get a much better handle on its customer base. At the management level, a training programme was launched to help managers become more effective leaders.

The main consequences of this buzz of activity were that employees were confused, stressed out and working long hours. Furthermore, the leaders took their eyes off the basics of the business. Early on, I posed some questions to the CEO:

- Are all these initiatives doable?

- Can we stop two or three of them or at least delay them?

- What are the implications if we postpone them?

The CEO decided to postpone the changes that were primarily operational issues. This problem is deep-rooted in corporations. Leadership gets so deep into initiatives that nobody stops to ask the million-dollar question: Is this doable? Once the financial commitment has been made, the momentum builds and some progress has been made, people stop asking that question.

I'm reminded of the bride-to-be who belatedly realises that her betrothed is not the right person for her, but marches down the aisle anyway, because the arrangements are too far in progress. Be the lone voice of reason in the wilderness. Have the courage to ask the basic questions, such as: Can this business succeed on all these fronts at once? Challenge your own thinking and challenge that of others.

If you are leading by starting too many initiatives, you can expect that your team are doing the same. New projects and goals will proliferate. Change is good, but too much too fast confuses everybody. The results are certain to disappoint. Soon the organisation will spin out of control or be paralysed by indecision about priorities.

My experience has shown me that the best-performing companies implement only three or four initiatives a year. Otherwise, your message to your troops gets diluted, and you are setting yourself and your organisation up for failure on a daily basis.

A leading manufacturer hired me to coach its top leadership teams. When I examined the organisation closely, I discovered that it had an astonishing 80 different sets of consulting companies in its employ – each with its own agenda and ideas about how the CEO should be running the place. There was no coordinated effort between the consultancies. Not surprisingly, chaos reigned.

The most recently hired consultancy was assigned the duty of rationalising the company's extensive use of consultants! No wonder the CEO and top leaders felt burdened. I encouraged the CEO to focus on a small number of projects that we determined could be executed in the business and would make a significant difference in the company.

Million-dollar Question

If you fell under a bus, what would happen to your company?

Your answer to that million-dollar question serves as a barometer for whether you are focusing on the right things or spinning your wheels. When I ask that question, almost every person I coach admits that he or she has failed to groom a successor, or, for that matter, even identify one.

Figuring out who could follow in your footsteps needs be to moved high up on your list of priorities. Force yourself to think about what your successor would learn from watching you as you go about your daily activities. That's a good exercise to make sure you stay on target.

Stop and Reflect

Think about which three activities really matter today.

Add up the time it would take to complete all the items on today's to-do list, add on meeting time, and add on time for unexpected additions. What is the total? I'm willing to bet that it far exceeds the 24 hours we're all granted in a day. If you could do only three things today, what would they be and why?

> **Leadership Note:** *Leaders who do less but do more of the right things are more effective.*

Lots of leaders operate under a delusion. They tell themselves, If only I can get to the end of this month, this week, this project, (or whatever), then I'll

- spend more time with my family;

- have more time to think;

- leave the office earlier; or

- be less busy.

Those nearest and dearest to them know that's a myth, irrespective of the promises and goals their partners offer up, such as:

- just let me get to the next holiday;

- just let me hire a chief operations officer; or

- just let me finish this project.

Million-dollar Question

Are you routinely breaking promises to yourself and your family regarding your schedule?

Top-tier leaders don't *intend* to leave a string of broken promises trailing behind them where their loved ones are concerned. They sit, however, in the middle of a dynamic system. Some might call it a maelstrom. In reality, by the time many people have finished everything on their plate, and even if they did not generate a single additional to-do item personally, another one hundred items would be in the place of those just dispensed. An avalanche of emails keeps coming, their presence is required at more and more meetings, competitors are shifting tactics, and they must respond.

Stop and Reflect

You must take breaks and give yourself space to be inspired and energised.

You need look no further than professional athletes to explode the myth that round-the-clock hard work delivers the best results. Pacing is a critical part of sports training. Business leaders, however, get in a cycle of setting impossible expectations of themselves. Any sports coach or executive coach will tell you the feeling that you're not making progress is debilitating. Yet CEOs and senior executives set themselves up to fail on a daily basis by chasing after the urgent rather than the important.

> **Leadership Note:** *A leader must create breathing room on a daily basis, which may mean limiting the to-do list to those three activities that really matter.*

I call it practising corporate yoga. Otherwise, great ideas will be squeezed out and will never have the space to sprout wings. When your nose is pressed to the grindstone all you see is the grindstone. You can't look up and see the big picture and provide the vision your organisation needs.

Wake-up Call

**Being clear on what you are *not* going to do
is as important as what you *are* going to do.**

A new whiz-kid CEO was just six weeks into her job as boss of a billion-pound global business, and almost everything in the business needed fixing. She was in danger of being dragged into parts of the operation that didn't deserve her focus. We worked on a *not*-to-do list as well as a to-do list for her first 90 days on the job.

Countless CEOs with whom I'd worked had found that the consistent discipline of identifying only three must-do things – the three things that will have the biggest effect on their business and team – constituted a turning point in their careers.

So in a coaching session with the whiz-kid who was continually stretched beyond her limit, I asked, 'Are you up for a game?'

With her competitive nature, I knew she couldn't resist a challenge. 'Other than meetings you must attend, here are the rules: I want you to agree to decide on three items a day that only you can do really well and uniquely to help the business,' I said.

'You must do those three items each day, no matter what. If you get other things done, too, that's OK, but the three items you pick as must-dos take precedence.'

I further explained that numerous CEOs with whom I've worked declared this technique to be revolutionary in their work lives. 'Do it first thing when you arrive for the day and do it consistently,' I urged.

She still looked dubious. 'If you don't think it's working well by the end of the week, you can quit the game,' I said reassuringly. After a long pause, she agreed to my terms, and we shook hands on the deal.

The first time we did this exercise, the three things she elected to do were (1) phone her most important client and have a conversation about whether they were happy with the service her firm was providing; (2) get the two leaders of two important functions in the business that weren't working well together into her office to discuss the problems and how to resolve them; and (3) spend an hour thinking about the outcomes she wanted for a sales conference that was scheduled for two months hence.

None of the three took long, but for different reasons each item on her top-three list was very important to the success of the business. First, from her talks with her most important client she discovered some areas of vulnerability in the business. She also found out what they particularly liked and was able to reinforce that with her own people.

Next, she had to deal with the heads of two functions in the business – sales and marketing – who refused to work effectively together, and the disconnect was costing the business significantly. Although she didn't like dealing with conflict, sorting out the issues was critical.

As for the sales event, the 800-strong sales staff got together only once a year, and she would be opening and closing the meeting, which carried a £1-million-plus price tag. Although she knew it was an extraordinarily important event, she kept putting off thinking about it in favour of dealing with the urgent. Once she agreed to move it to the top of her list, she had plenty of time to structure the event to get the maximum impact.

What did she eliminate? Piles of magazines – *Business Week*, *Fortune*, *Forbes* and the like – were stacked in her cluttered office. She kept intending to read them, but never got around to the task. She assigned someone to read them for her and flag anything that might be important to the business.

She ended the practice of having her staff submit drafts of their meeting agendas for her blessing. Most of these meetings were operational ones that she wasn't even planning to attend.

She stopped attending breakfast network meetings with other CEOs, because she was spending an inordinate amount of time at them when they had really added little to her business over the years.

Million-dollar Question

Are you letting old habits drain your valuable time?

On her to-do list, she also had 'choose office furniture' lingering for several months. She kept intending to go through furniture brochures, but never got around to it. She agreed to let someone in the corporate-affairs office who knew her taste and what image the business was trying to portray go through the stack of brochures that had been on her desk for weeks. 'Give me two suggestions and I'll pick one,' she said.

Old habits can also drain valuable time. As a former finance director and an accountant, this CEO loved numbers and used to go through financial management reports line by line. 'What are you paying your finance director for?' I asked. She agreed to let the finance team indicate anything that required her attention.

Finally, she knocked off her to-do list a number of people she thought she should see individually – mainly financial analysts and financial press people – which would have eaten up a huge chunk of time. She decided to invite these groups of people to a lunch, which was a far more efficient way to handle the meetings.

At the end of the week, we met for dinner. She entered the restaurant in a great mood, laughing as she approached the table. 'I was scared and tempted to say, "No, I won't play," ' she confessed. 'But I didn't want to admit it. I was also reassured when you told me other CEOs had played your game.'

'What was the outcome?' I asked.

'Funny thing is, I've done a lot less, but I've been more effective than ever in my role this week. That's not just my perception, either. Several colleagues gave me feedback that for the first time since I got this position they saw me as on top of the job rather than lagging behind. I wasn't running around like a chicken with its head cut off.'

Stop and Reflect

Ask yourself this: 'What am I doing each day that, in the final analysis, doesn't really matter?'

I asked her if she noted any cost to our game. She replied, 'The only thing I lost was my guilt at not doing more. This exercise opened my eyes to the fact that a lot of what I was doing before did not matter.'

Still, the CEO had to make a significant adjustment in her go-go-go, do-do-do mindset. In fact, she told me that, at the midway point on Wednesday night, she had dinner with her family for the first time in weeks. 'I told my husband that I thought doing more by doing less was a great idea in theory, but I didn't think I'd be able to stick to it,' she said.

Her husband replied, 'You've never been a quitter, and I can already see a difference in you.' That spot of encouragement spurred her on.

Even leaders running multinational, multibillion-pound/dollar corporations sometimes have a big blind spot: they are not efficient at self-management. Their meetings routinely run over by half an hour or more; they overpromise and underdeliver; their to-do lists are too long. In my many one-on-one sessions with top leaders, I've often been struck by the difference between what they think they should do and what they actually do.

Following are some of the most common 'shoulds' I hear:

- hold the vision and mission out front;

- influence corporate culture;

- put a public face on the business for the press, analysts and other outsiders;

- formulate a clear and well-communicated strategy;

- be out and about in the business with employees and customers.

By contrast, here's what most are actually doing:

- spending their time sequestered in meetings with other senior-level executives;

- managing day-to-day details too much;

- starting too many new initiatives;

- spreading themselves too thinly across too many projects;

- being invisible to their employees and customers.

Wake-up Call

Within a month you can form a new habit.

Sometimes CEOs are unaware of how their time is being used, and most are unrealistic about how long different projects take. I ask clients to tell me where they think they spend their time, and I have them write it down. Then I ask, 'Where should your time be going, given your role and where you add value?' For a week they track where it's actually going, and the results are often revealing.

Once we ruthlessly eliminate the endless meetings, needless to-dos and unnecessary reading material from their schedules, my clients find huge scope for making adjustments. I've had several CEOs report that they opened up as much as 40 per cent of their schedule. They find more than enough time to get to the important items on their freshly trimmed list of to-dos.

If you decide to play the 'three must-dos a day' game, let someone know what you are doing, and then conduct an in-depth review of the results of your week with that person. What support system do you need to make that happen? Enlist your personal assistant's help. Put a screensaver on your computer or a sign on your desk to remind you of your commitment. Send a trusted person an email at the end of each day to tell them whether you accomplished your three things.

A few examples of the questions I ask my clients are these:

- What was the upside?

- What's not working?

- Was there any cost?

- Do you want to keep this game going?

- If so, it's vital to build on the success of the first week.

Changing behaviour is not an easy thing to do. If you do your top three must-do tasks consistently for a week, what would you love to do? It may sound a little corny, but rewarding yourself can help you stay on track. Buy some CDs you've wanted or treat yourself to a spa getaway. Whatever will help you stay motivated, do it.

Bear in mind that, when the pressure is on again, we tend to fall back on our old coping mechanisms. The key is quickly to review how the new tactic of focusing on three things a day is working. Within a month, you will have formed a new habit.

Wake-up Call

Rooting out your negative behaviour.

What of the poor, overburdened managing partner in a professional-services firm with 120 items on his mental to-do list? I gradually got him down to three items a day, but initially he was too fearful of losing control. It was too big a step for him.

Early on in our coaching sessions, I teased him that he was the easiest top-level executive to get on the telephone that I'd ever coached. 'What do you mean?' he asked.

'If I phone you at 6 am or 11 pm, there's nobody else in the office, and you pick up the phone,' I said.

At weekends he took home mountains of paperwork, most of which he returned on Monday unread. He nearly drove his wife mad when I finally persuaded him to take a weekend holiday. He sat by the pool with a mobile phone and laptop.

He finally got serious about taking the Three Must-do Challenge when his wife threatened divorce because he took one too many calls on his mobile phone. This one happened to be in the maternity ward of the hospital while his wife was having their first child.

I always encourage people I'm coaching to identify the cause of their negative behaviour. What leads people to have 120 items on their to-do list? Fear is the root of most of the out-of-control agendas I encounter

- fear of failure;

- fear of forgetting something; and

- fear of letting go (resulting in inadequate delegation).

I also often see

- lack of focus: the leader is not really clear on what's most important in his or her role, so the person has no filters;

- lack of planning: if you don't think through things, your agenda will be littered with random actions;

- lack of or inadequate delegation;

- lack of trust in other people; and

- lack of self-awareness.

> **Leadership Note:** *Perceptions are important – your hard work may be mistaken for an uncaring attitude.*

In this leader's case, his conditioning from both his parents was that the secret to success was to work harder than anybody else. He honestly believed that there was a direct correlation between the number of hours you put in and the success you have.

Because he always had his head down, buried in his work, people never saw him and thought him uncaring. He was perceived within the organisation as being uninterested in the business, despite all the long hours he put in. To counter that perception, he made spending an hour walking around the office chatting with employees one of his top three priorities. It drove him crazy initially, because it is hard to measure the value of that directly.

The company's staff turnover rate had reached an alarming level. He decided for the first week that every day he would send a thank-you note to employees for something he'd noticed. That was not something he would naturally do or that would show up on his to-do list, but he admitted he understood the high value that this seemingly small task could have.

The feedback that he got from his employees and peers was that his firm didn't communicate a clear vision. His isolated way of working had left people with no sense of what his vision for the business was. He agreed to prepare an 'elevator speech' – the kind of thing you can communicate in a two-minute ride in a lift – what the business does and where it's going.

All three of these things (spending time with employees, writing thank-you notes and clarifying the corporate vision) weren't naturally of high importance to this man, but our coaching work transformed them into the obvious must-dos.

Million-dollar Question

What message are you sending your employees, shareholders and customers by your actions?

Most employees would answer that their leaders are overworked and have no time for them. Ironically, most CEOs paint too rosy a picture about the future.

They come across as overconfident, and therefore shareholders perceive them as unbelievable.

Sadly, most customers would say leaders' actions come through loud and clear, but the message they are communicating is: we're not interested in you or what you think about our service or product.

Wake-up Call

**People want to follow good leaders.
Lead a life worthy of imitation.**

Not long ago, I had one of the most bizarre conversations of my coaching career with a top CEO.

'I have to ask you something,' I said. 'I've wanted to ask it for the last three meetings.'

'What's that?'

'Why do you, a captain of industry, the head of one of the largest Fortune 100 companies, a legend in the business world, have a missing button on your jacket?'

'I'm so busy that I haven't got time to deal with that sort of trivia.'

'I'm going to put "fix jacket" on your to-do list from this coaching session, and I will review with you at our next meeting.'

On the surface, my concern over his missing button might appear counterintuitive to what I've just been preaching. However, this CEO was sending the wrong message to everyone he encountered by not taking the time to fix a niggling problem.

To his employees, he was signalling that work was so demanding that they should not dare to take a few moments to take care of personal needs. After all, if the big boss was so hurried, what right did *they* have to take time out to attend to basic personal matters? More ominously, to outsiders, the CEO's lack of attention to that detail might have caused them to wonder, If he'd ignore the small problems, what else might be lurking?

Million-dollar Question

What's the equivalent of missing buttons in your life?

My point is that everything you do – or don't do – is examined in all quarters. People are going to examine everything about you – from the way you dress to your speech patterns to what pictures and books are in your office. That makes some leaders uncomfortable, but, if you are a leader, people are going to follow you.

What are the mouldy oldies in *your* work or personal life that are draining your energy? In the grand scheme of things they may not be important, but sometimes you have to clear the psychic clutter in order to move ahead. What keeps reappearing on your to-do list? Maybe it's a broken blind in your office. Maybe it's learning how to work the phone system and transfer calls on the odd occasion one comes to you that shouldn't have. Maybe it's a persistent irritation with your personal assistant. Take the five minutes to clear up those items that nag at you.

One CEO of a retail company often worked after his personal assistant had left for the evening, and he was often frustrated because he didn't understand the logic of the PA's filing system. But he had never taken the five minutes to get her to explain it to him. It never got high enough up on the list, yet he was annoyed with the time wasted hunting for papers on a regular basis. A five-minute conversation took care of the problem.

Stop and Reflect

Name the six things that irritate you the most. Get them fixed! You don't have to do it yourself, but get them taken care of now!

After I've worked with a leader for a while, we create what I call 'Rules for Winning'. The rules are based on what they have learned that help them perform at an optimal level while doing less. Each set of rules is personal.

Here are my personal Rules for Winning:

1. Always start my day with the top three things I need to accomplish.

2. Ask my personal assistant for feedback once a week on how I'm doing in terms of time management.

3. Screen all my mobile-phone calls before answering.

Ask yourself, what have I learned that, if I kept doing them, would enable me to be my best? Write down your rules and keep them handy.

Executive Summary

Million-dollar Questions

- If you did one thing that would move you towards accomplishing your most important goal, what would it be?

- If you fell under a bus, what would happen to your company?

- Are you routinely breaking promises to yourself and your family regarding your schedule?

- Are you letting old habits drain your valuable time?

- What message are you sending your employees, shareholders and customers by your actions?

- What's the equivalent of missing buttons in your life?

Stop and Reflect

- Begin the process of trimming that to-do list by accepting that you are not superhuman.

- Think about which three activities really matter today.

- You must take breaks and give yourself space to be inspired and energised.

- Ask yourself this: 'What am I doing each day that, in the final analysis, doesn't really matter?'

- Name the six things that irritate you the most. Get them fixed! You don't have to do it yourself, but get them taken care of now!

Wake-up calls

- Do not add to your agenda unless you drop something else.

- Being clear on what you are *not* going to do is as important as what you *are* going to do.

- Within a month you can form a new habit.

- Rooting out your negative behaviour.

- People want to follow good leaders. Lead a life worthy of imitation.

Leadership Notes

- Businesses and leaders reduce their own effectiveness when they attempt too much.

- Leaders who do less but do more of the right things are more effective.

- A leader must create breathing space on a daily basis, which may mean limiting the to-do list to those three activities that really matter.

- Perceptions are important – your hard work may be mistaken for an uncaring attitude.

What can only you do?

WHAT IS THE UNIQUE VALUE *you* – just you – bring to the business? As we saw in the past chapter, you must be clear every day about the three things you can do – on that day – that will add the most to the business. Identify those three things day in and day out, and you'll be amazed at what takes place in your business and your life. It takes incredible discipline to think about those things and act upon them. Do your top-three list with precision.

I keep a list of all my tasks on my laptop. I never try to remember anything. That keeps my mind clear. Each day I look at the list, focusing on my top three items. Once a week, I scan the entire list to make sure that my daily top three always represent my highest-return items. On a daily basis, I also reflect on my personal mission. For 2004 it was 'be fit and flush', which meant concentrating on my health and organising my finances.

Now that you've identified your top three most important tasks each day, how do you believe your life will change if you keep doing these things? Promise you'll do your three highest-priority tasks no matter what. Then keep your word to yourself.

Wake-up Call

Do not turn your life into one big to-do list.

Many leaders find focusing on what is truly important difficult, because doing is so much easier than thinking. They are easily distracted by details rather than focusing on the company's overall strategy. Still, other leaders stumble in this regard, because they are fearful of letting go. At all costs, avoid doing what other people in your organisation should be doing. You disempower your people when you do that.

Leaders are often unaware of where their time goes. Think about top-performing athletes for a moment: they are highly aware of what things they need to do to perform their best – right down to what and when to eat. I often ask someone I'm coaching, 'Tell me where you think you spend your time in a week.'

I'll get an answer: six hours in strategy meetings, ten hours talking to customers, three hours dealing with emails, and so on. Then I ask, 'Where should your time be going given your role and where you add value?'

For a week they track where their time is actually going. Invariably, this exercise is revealing, and hardly anyone is on target with where they think they are spending their time. In fact, most leaders are not only out of touch with how they are using their time, they are also unrealistic about how long tasks or meetings will take. I see many four-hour meetings stretch to five, six or even seven hours.

Million-dollar Question

What's your plan for action?

A global pharmaceutical company hired a hot new CEO. He had a strong performance record on the financial side and was an excellent marketer, too. That made him the right one to send to the underperforming region and turn it around.

Together we outlined his plan: assemble a great team, get a grasp on the financials, redevelop the marketing strategy, and press the flesh.

Stop and Reflect

Separate the important from the urgent.

We decided he should spend 15 per cent of his time introducing himself throughout the market, which he didn't enjoy doing because that isn't natural to him, but he understood it was necessary. The rest *was* natural for him – he could build teams and handle financials and strategies in his sleep.

At six months, I sometimes offer a review. We look at successes and disappointments, at what's working and what isn't. I ask about lessons learned.

In his case, he reported nothing but success. He'd hit all his goals, and he had the data to prove it – except for the 15 per cent of his time he said he was out and about. I asked if his personal assistant could put together numbers that would summarise his out-of-office time. She came back with a surprise: it wasn't 15 per cent, it was 7 per cent.

His gut feeling had convinced him otherwise.

Stop and Reflect

Beware of assumptions and beware of attempting changes that are too big.

We agreed again about the importance of his visibility throughout his market – that its importance outweighed other financial and strategic urgencies. Especially now that the business was turning around, he needed to be seen.

Still, when he said he planned to double the original goal to 30 per cent, I had to talk him down. Quadrupling an effort is almost always unachievable. Better to shoot for incremental increases and give himself time.

Wake-up Call

Find the bottlenecks that are keeping you from the next level.

A director of strategy who asked me to help her get organised had a bigger mess in mind: shattering the glass ceiling.

She said she wanted me to help her organise her burgeoning workload. But when, in our first meeting, I asked her a couple of questions about her aspirations, the truth slipped out.

'I'd love to be COO.'

'What are you doing about that?' I asked.

'Oh, I'm doubtful it could happen. No woman has been COO here before. It's probably not realistic.'

'I have an idea,' I said. 'Let's keep talking about what you really want for your career while we deal with your workload issues.'

Million-dollar Question

What greatness could you achieve if you focused on it?

I wondered whether she was doing everything possible to maximise her chances of landing that role. When I asked her in broad terms where she was spending her time, she said she was completely focused on doing the strategy job as well as it could be done. Many people believe that their best shot at advancement comes from doing their current job extremely well and waiting to get noticed.

Almost all of them are still waiting.

I suggested she consider taking two steps towards that dream by answering the following questions. First, how should she develop herself to be ready for the COO position? Second, who were the champions at the top of the organisation who could pull for her to win that kind of advancement? She should start networking with those people.

'But with my workload, where am I supposed to find the time for self-development and networking?' she asked.

Million-dollar Question

What on your to-do list today, if not done, would have catastrophic consequences for the business?

Suddenly, we had an incentive to drive the reorganisation of her workload. More efficiency in her strategy job would give her time to cultivate her COO dream.

We agreed to tackle the workflow bottlenecks: paperwork, emails, meetings and telephone calls. Here's what she did about each one:

- *Paperwork.* Instead of carrying home a load of financial press each weekend, she handed the stack to one of her team members. He got the benefit of reviewing newspapers and magazines from the financial world, and she saved time by scanning the points of interest he clipped for her.

- *Email.* She spent only the first few minutes of the day reading and responding to the most critical correspondence. Her personal assistant screened the rest.

- *Meetings.* She assigned the role of note taker to a team member and made her responsible for summarising the decisions, actions required, calendar items and follow-up schedules.

Finally, she booked time with herself every Friday – quality, un-interruptible think time for reading and report writing.

As the changes took shape, her workload dropped 20 per cent. The extra hours she gained she put to good use, pursuing her dream.

Six months later, she sent me a very nice bottle of champagne with a note attached: 'I got it!'

Wake-up Call

Decide what's the highest and best use of yourself.

One of the United States' strongest consumer brands slipped from first to fourth in the field, revealing strategic failures and faltering management. A new CEO was named.

I met with him in the interval before he started the position. He said he wanted me to coach him for the first year.

'What do you expect from me as your coach?'

'Be ruthless. Challenge me constantly about where I'm spending my time and focusing my attention, because I suspect I'll discover many more problems and issues than we already know about.'

We decided on a refocusing question, a mantra: 'Is this the highest and best use of me?' As his coach, I took on the role of keeping that question in front of him, helping him decide where his efforts would get the biggest results – and reminding him to set the small stuff aside.

> **Leadership Note:** *The person on top has to be on top of the job.*

We met weekly. He found all the problems he had expected and more, and I kept the 'best use' question in his face.

Three months after he started, we surveyed the staff, which had good news: he was nailing the big issues and the must-dos. The business was turning around.

The employees especially liked what his leadership was doing for morale. Where the previous CEO randomly fired in all directions while sinking, now the man on top was on top of his job. The whole company could see it.

Stop and Reflect

Every day ask yourself: What are the three things that only I can do that will add the most to the business? What are the three things that would improve my personal life?

Six months in, he delivered a keynote talk to business analysts and the financial press. He described the six most important challenges the company faced and exactly what he was doing about them. After his frank presentation and hard evidence of real change, they were glowing with affirmation.

Wake-up Call

**Do not allow your strength
to become your weakness.**

Anything done to excess can tip the balance of your life. Even a good characteristic can be a problem if you rely on it to excess.

A charismatic CEO had a great open-door policy, and people loved it. He was always available and ready to listen. Every day he demonstrated how he truly cared about the people who worked for him.

When I'm looking at the CEO's relationships in a company, I often begin with the personal assistant. I asked the PA in this case to tell me something she thought the CEO should stop doing, something he should start and something he ought to continue. She hardly drew a breath. 'I wish he'd stop being available all the time.'

Stop the thing he was good at? I asked her why. 'He's available all the time!' she said, sounding exasperated. 'People are in and out of his office all day. Some of it's important. A lot of it's ridiculous. There's no filter!'

I wondered whether the CEO knew about the wisdom sitting outside his office door. 'Have you ever said this to him?'

'I thought about it, but I'd just be one more person barging in.'

I suggested we have an informal conversation with him and asked her to share with him exactly what she had told me. He got it immediately, but was worried about the remedy. 'If I suddenly stop being available, I'm slamming my door in a lot of faces.'

The PA had a solution: 'Let me block out your calendar and post a schedule of your open-door time. And, while I'm at it, I'll start screening your emails, too.'

One thing that CEO should continue? Keep that personal assistant.

Million-dollar Question

What is your unique added value and are you bringing it to the table?

The consensus-building CEO liked what he heard: people had a sense of ownership in decisions.

'Are there downsides to consensus building?' I asked. When consensus building runs wild, outcomes walk the plank for the sake of agreement.

The CEO said the process made people happy. 'Look how involved they are!'

The people said they often wondered about the CEO's opinion and wanted to hear it because he had a long and admirable track record in the industry. 'He's the CEO, but we don't have a clue what he thinks.'

> **Leadership Note:** *Popularity is nice, but make sure you accomplish your mission.*

I offered three ideas. First, it's not a genuine consensus if any views are suppressed. Second, people who want to know what their CEO thinks should ask. And, third, CEOs can tell people their opinions even when they're not asked.

Everyone agreed.

Wake-up Call

It pays to know when the little things count.

While I was coaching the CEO of an office products company, I sat in on a management meeting to observe the process. It went well, I thought, except for one item on the agenda.

Does the format for the company's holiday party warrant 20 minutes of the 20-member executive management team's time? I asked the CEO why he added the topic to his agenda.

'Two reasons,' he said. 'First, the people in this meeting are the most influential on the workforce. If they can take the time to talk about the kind of perk that makes people feel good about their jobs, that sends a message.'

The company had just merged, and it was smart to help the workforce feel good about the new company.

'Second, I wanted the people in the meeting, who come from both companies, to get to know each other and discuss their former cultures. Before we move on to the big issues, let's practise talking, listening and finding a mutually satisfying decision.'

Good call. An excellent tactical use of party planning!

Million-dollar Question

What action or conversations are you avoiding that could make a big difference in your business/life?

Wake-up Call

Sometimes it's wise to break with protocol.

A leading Pacific Rim company had me working with team leaders from various Asian countries as they developed projects. My role was to keep the teams collaborating and sharing their best practices rather than retreating into national silos.

In contrast with that noble intent, the president of the company was carefully isolated. His assistant zealously controlled access to him, determined meeting agendas and issued rulings on what questions the president would hear.

As fate would have it, one of the teams had a critical issue that needed the president's attention. The assistant had already scrubbed the topic from the agenda, but the need for action remained.

So I asked the team, 'Who's willing to break protocol? Who will say, "I know this isn't on the agenda, but there's a crucial issue that the heads of the countries want to bring to your attention"?'

A team member who had worked with the president in another business reluctantly agreed to the challenge. He recognised the risk to his career, but we all could see that the issues were too important to walk away from. The team also expressed their weariness with the president's inaccessibility. To fulfil their objectives, they needed more direct interaction with him. This was the time to start.

The meeting came. The challenge was issued: 'I know this isn't on the agenda, but there's a crucial issue that the heads of the countries want to bring to your attention.'

Million-dollar Question

What are you missing by relying on only the formal lines of communication?

And the dreaded result? Anger from the assistant and hearty enthusiasm from the president. Not only did he understand the issues, but he would attend the next team meeting to talk them through.

And the brave executive who broke protocol won brownie points. Not long after that, the president had a new assistant.

Unfortunately, senior managers often don't hear everything they need to hear. Staff inadvisably protect them from bad news. As a leader, get out and about and talk to the people. If you just rely on the formal lines of communication and review meetings, by no means are you guaranteed the full picture.

An action step that often comes out of coaching is to have a conversation that you have been afraid to have or have been putting off for other reasons. With a domineering leader in the picture, there are often a number of topics that languish, because people are afraid to bring them up.

Wake-up Call

Don't hold back.

Like redeeming a two-for-one coupon, the board of directors of a deeply troubled telecommunications firm picked a chairman and a CEO at the same time – a risky, unusual move as far as continuity is concerned. Dire circumstances, however, require decisive action.

Although both had deep experience in telecommunications, the problems in the far-flung organisation were grave. They were given six months to fix the company, and asked for my help in crafting a plan. For my part, I started with the question, 'What are your perceptions of the state of the business?' I asked that because it's important to be clear on the *what* before digging into the *how*.

> ## Million-dollar Question _____
>
> What is the unique value you bring to the business?

In this first meeting with the two of them, they described their shared view of the challenges. 'It looks like you're absolutely on the same page about what's working and what's not in this business,' I said.

Then I posed the least asked, but perhaps one of the most vital, questions in business: 'How do you feel about the tasks you face?'

Even though the business world seems almost exclusively left-brained, analytical and rational, the people who work there have feelings and emotions, which affect how they do their work.

Wake-up Call

**Allow doubts, fears, excitement and
other emotions that you experience in
regard to your job to come to the surface.**

They both talked about great anxiety, because there was so much wrong with the business and they had so little time to turn it around. At the same time, they were invigorated by the challenge that the board laid at their feet and understood the chance they had to be 'white knights'.

Their answers led to the next question: 'Given the mixture of anxiety and excitement you say you feel, what stands out?'

'The enormity of what must be done,' they both answered. The company had gone through a number of mergers and now had multiple locations in cities across the United States.

From that, a bold idea emerged. Instead of assuming traditional roles in which the CEO executes the one-year operating plan operating while the chairman tends to shareholders, analysts and long-range strategy, these two decided to become joint chiefs. Their reasoning was indisputable: if day-to-day operations weren't improved, there was no 'long range' to strategise for.

After comparing their strengths and weaknesses, they parcelled out responsibilities accordingly. For the next year, they worked as a CEO duo, pouring their resources into short-term recovery goals for the business. The chairman let the business press and shareholders know that he would have little contact with them for six months while he focused his attention completely on the turnaround.

Over the next several months, I coached them, making sure they remained joined at the hip, communicating about and maintaining clarity in their responsibilities.

After that year, with the successful turnaround in the bag, they reverted to the more classic roles of CEO and chairman.

> **Leadership Note:** *Your time is your most valuable resource. Look for ways to maximise your time and your enjoyment of it.*

All of us can get locked into a mindset that certain things about our lives are impossible to change. Sometimes it takes someone looking at our schedules with fresh eyes to help us see the options.

Wake-up Call

A change of address can change your life.

The senior partner in a large estate agency had a dream house in the country, but the commute to his London office was a nightmare. He hired a driver and worked en route, but invariably arrived at his office irritable and bad-tempered and just couldn't wait for the weekends. So I asked him, 'Have you considered a flat?'

He looked thunderstruck. He had never considered such a thing.

'You could take a flat near your office,' I explained, letting it sink in. 'You could work four days intensively in London, then work from home on Fridays.' He was smiling. I went on, 'And I'll bet your wife would enjoy visiting you in the city. A little shopping? Dinner out?'

Fifteen years later I ran into him. 'That change made the biggest difference in our lives,' he said. 'Thank you again.'

> **Leadership Note:** *Know the difference between* organising *your life and* dancing *with life.*

Wake-up Call

When you need help, *get* help.

I once had a CEO tell me that one of his employees was working too hard. The man was in charge of the company's sophisticated trade show displays and, show after show, he performed his duties with vigour. It was great for sales and market visibility, but the CEO was concerned that the trade shows weren't part of a long-range strategy and that, driven by his perfectionist streak, the man running the shows was working too hard.

I visited this trade show manager. He agreed that the shows weren't integrated into a strategic plan, but, as for overworking, he couldn't get the point.

'The way I work is 110 per cent. That's me doing my share. You can't ask me to do less than I feel I ought to. Besides, what would the competitors say if the quality of what we do suddenly dropped?'

'Then how about delegating some of the responsibility?' I asked him. 'Share the load.'

'Sure, but nobody else knows this like I do. If I have to train someone, that means more time. You just said I should do less than 110 per cent.'

That was the catch. He already had more than enough to do. And he was the only person with the expertise to train his assistant.

> **Leadership Note:** *People are capable and have enormous untapped potential. Let them use it.*

I asked him to take a longer view. 'Pick two people with the capability to take over from you someday. Then let's try a different approach to the train-your-own-successor problem.'

He selected his people, and we agreed they would shadow him through his preparations for the next show. They would learn just by watching. After the show, he set aside a week to meet with them and debrief. And finally, to get the benefit of observing how other companies ran their trade shows, summer associates were dispatched with video cameras. Their footage served as executive summaries for the trainees.

The plan worked. In time, two new managers could capably share trade-show responsibilities with him. And he never had to drop a percentage point from his 110 per cent effort. He still works 110 per cent – that's his nature – but it's less demanding and stressful now.

Stop and Reflect

Give it away. Identify three areas of responsibility and ten places in which you are involved to give away.

Reorganising your time is not always as easy as making a decision. In the case I've just described, part of what made getting him to parcel out some of the load so difficult was that his inner drive to give 110 per cent was hardwired into him. Trying to change that would have heightened his anxiety and stress.

One-size-fits-all coaching doesn't work. If I coach a person to stop checking emails from their laptop while on holiday, it might actually produce more anxiety for that person than if they took one hour a day to check emails and phone the office. Look for what will work in your life.

Ask yourself constantly what only YOU can do. Then decide what you don't *have* to do. Can it be delegated? Will the company still function as effectively if you – you personally – no longer perform those tasks? Might SHEDDING SOME DUTIES actually improve things, by allowing you to concentrate more on strategy and less on operational matters? Sometimes, remember, doing less is doing more.

Executive Summary

Million-dollar Questions

- Ask yourself: What's your plan for action?

- What greatness could you achieve if you focused on it?

- What on your to-do list today, if not done, would have catastrophic consequences for the business?

- What is your unique added value and are you bringing it to the table?

- What action or conversations are you avoiding that could make a big difference in your business/life?

- What are you missing by relying on only the formal lines of communication?

- What is the unique value you bring to the business?

Stop and Reflect

- Separate the important from the urgent.

- Beware of assumptions and beware of attempting changes that are too big.

- Every day ask yourself: What are the three things that only I can do that will add the most to the business? What are the three things that would improve my personal life?

- Give it away. Identify three areas of responsibility and ten places in which you are involved to give away.

Wake-up Calls

- Do not turn your life into one big to-do list.

- Find the bottlenecks that are keeping you from the next level.

- Decide what's the highest and best use of yourself.

- Do not allow your strength to become your weakness.

- It pays to know when the little things count.

- Sometimes it's wise to break with protocol.

- Don't hold back.

- Allow doubts, fears, excitement and other emotions that you experience in regard to your job to come to the surface.

- A change of address can change your life.

- When you need help, *get* help.

Leadership Notes

- The person on top has to be on top of the job.

- Popularity is nice, but make sure you accomplish your mission.

- Your time is your most valuable resource. Look for ways to maximise your time and your enjoyment of it.

- Know the difference between *organising* your life and *dancing* with life.

- People are capable and have enormous untapped potential. Let them use it.

Would you do anything differently if you knew you had only a year to live?

MANY TOP LEADERS HAVE BEEN conditioned to believe that if only they could work harder and harder, they'd be more successful. They get addicted to operating in this fashion. As a result, vital parts of their lives atrophy from neglect – family life, friendships, spirituality, recreation and their physical bodies.

Ironically, I often find the higher up the corporate ladder the leader I am coaching has ascended, the more that person's work–life balance is dangerously out of kilter. If you are tempted to skip over this chapter, that should be a warning signal.

I urge you to give serious thought to the question posed in this chapter heading. I guarantee your priorities will come sharply into focus if you do. We all need reminders of what's really important from time to time.

In Greek times, great value was put on making time for contemplation. Work was secondary. These days work is given great meaning. Indeed, I've yet to meet a leader who needed help spending more time at work. However, many top level executives have, in a sense, resigned from their other roles in life. High performers get shackled to the adrenalin high of success that comes from work. When they run into difficulties at home, for example, the temptation is to bury themselves at the office.

Stop and Reflect

Make the most of living life instead of mostly living with regrets.

Now that you've stated your priorities, where are the disconnects? For example, perhaps spending more time with your children rates high on your priority list. What do you do when a colleague schedules a meeting for late Friday afternoon? You know his meetings always run long, and you'll risk missing part of your son's football game if you attend. Examining those everyday decisions will show you whether you are living out your priorities.

Wake-up Call

Remember, you're at this point in your family relationships only once – this moment won't come back.

Twelve years into his job, the executive director of a large trade union and I were discussing the topic of how to use time most effectively. I asked, 'If you had your time again, what would you do differently?' Much to my surprise, this big burly man, who projected a macho image, started crying.

He replied, 'Hands down, I would have done something that I repeatedly said to myself I ought to do, and now it's too late – spend more time with my kids.'

Several months later, I visited this fellow at his beautiful beach house. Above the fireplace hung a huge painting of his three young children. He pointed to the painting and said, 'That was the age they were when I wished I'd spent more time with them.'

I said, 'You say it's too late, but is there anything you can do now?'

'It won't bring back the past, but I could sit down with each child individually and apologise.'

In our next session, he told me that he had followed through, and he made a commitment to his three kids that, if they had grandchildren, he wouldn't fall into the same trap.

Writing the answers to the following self-assessment will give you a snapshot of where you are:

1. What is my life all about?

2. What have been my biggest successes and disappointments during the past 12 months?

3. What are my strengths and weaknesses and how much time do I devote to the following areas?

- money/career

- health

- family

- leisure activities/hobbies

- friends/relationships

If all of your successes are in the money/career category, you know that your life is out of kilter. I can remember very few people who were completely satisfied with their work–life balance.

Doing this exercise will paint a clear picture of the current reality of your life. Now picture your ideal future state. What would you see, hear and feel? You won't be able to reach that ideal state unless you examine the thoughts and attitudes that led to the current state of affairs. What are the inner drivers that cause your behaviours? Changing how you live your life will take a stronger effort than making a decision to use your time differently.

Many of us have been conditioned to think that the harder we work, the more successful we will be. We have to challenge our inner beliefs with regard to time and work–life balance in order to make lasting changes.

Million-dollar Question

Is the ladder you're climbing up leaning against the right wall? What do you really want?

If you never change your work–life balance, will you be disappointed? A lot of people operate on the thought that it's just the current phase that is busier. They tell themselves, 'If I can just get to the end of this project, then I'll . . . ' The reason they keep getting so busy, however, is partly a reflection of the conditioning that will always lead them to overfill their cups.

This thought is also a myth, because we all live in a tidal wave of issues, emails, voicemails, competitors and the like that keep coming our way.

Stop and Reflect

The only person who can change the balance in your life is you.

Wake-up Call

Be bold and take a risk.

Would the world end if you gave yourself permission to go home at lunchtime for a meal with your partner?

An apocryphal story: after a late dinner with his wife, the CEO drives home past his office. There's a light on. It's 11.30.

His first thought is that someone has ignored the postings about energy savings. His second thought is to wonder whether somebody's actually still up there working.

Million-dollar Question

What kind of role model are you for your employees?

His third thought is curiosity about the kind of person who's willing to stay that late to get that much done. Finally, his thoughts darken as he wonders what kind of company requires so much from its workers that they have to stay that late.

If I go up and talk to him, the CEO asks himself, what will I say?

Stop and Reflect

What would your life partner or your children say was the most important thing in your life?

One CEO came to see me after his wife wrote this question on his birthday card: 'Are you married to me or the business?'

List what you are avoiding and what your life partner would say you are avoiding.

I was working my way through the management team at a high-tempo law firm, getting acquainted with the partners and finding out how I could help. One partner, in particular, described a heavy workload that followed him everywhere. In fact, he was always available to his clients and frequently on the phone – evenings, weekends, anywhere. He said his wife wasn't happy about this, but never more unhappy than recently. What was my opinion, he asked me.

'Well,' I said, 'let me ask you this: if you knew you only had a year to live, what would you change about the way you organise your life?'

His answer was immediate. 'I would restore my marriage and spend much more time with our new baby.'

I pointed out to him that he was actually telling me that he knew the difference between what was important in his life and what felt urgent. 'Your marriage and your child are truly important. When your mobile phone rings, that's an interruption you can decide about responding to.' Then I asked him again, 'So how about operating as if this were the last year of your life?'

'Easy to say,' he countered. But the more we talked, the more distressed he became about the deterioration in his marriage and the fact that he'd barely seen his six-month-old son.

'You're the only one who can change this,' I told him. 'It's up to you.'

We met again several days later, and I asked if he had decided what to do. He had another quick answer: 'I'm going to draw a line in the sand.'

'What do you mean by that?'

'I'm going to define clearly and absolutely what I will and what I won't give to my work life.' Then he made two promises. First, he would share openly with his wife where he'd drawn a line in the sand and would listen to her when she saw him stepping over it. Second, he wanted to meet me regularly for a year and include his wife in the sessions.

I don't often coach husbands and wives together but, frankly, I should offer to do it more often. Companies contract with me to coach their employees for performance improvements, but, if their marriages are struggling, some of the stress goes straight to the workplace. Why not deal with the marriage as part of the package?

In this case, it was the right move. I listened to the couple, noting their promises to each other, then acted as a conscience and reminded them of their agreements and commitments. While it never became the marriage from heaven, it certainly became less stressful for both of them. And he continued to be just as successful in his position as a partner in the law firm – a much happier partner.

> **Leadership Note:** *It helps to remember that you have only one life.*

I put the same question: 'If you only had one year to live, how would you organise your life?' to the managing director of a 40-unit chain of sandwich shops. Given her history of successes and her big plans for continued growth, I didn't expect her answer: 'If I only had a year to live, I'd sell out.'

I thought she'd explain how getting out of the business would give her more time with her family, but again she surprised me.

'I'd sell out because this is madness. We're a small chain going up against big competitors – it's like a little retailer facing off with Tesco. We might win, at least in the short term. But I'd be crazy to spend the last year of my life in that battle.'

I wondered whether she hadn't turned the life question into a strategic question. So I asked, 'If competition in this sector is that tough, is it smart to plough ahead with your growth plans?'

As we continued to talk, it became clear that the market had changed dramatically during the time she had expanded from one to 40 shops. Competitive forces were not the same – maybe her growth strategy needed revamping.

Her management team concurred and called for a consultant. And, in the end, the recommendation was exactly the same as the managing director answer to the first question: 'Sell out.'

For this managing director and her company, strategic clarity came with a new key question. Instead of just, 'What's the best way to run our business?' they also asked, 'And what's a better way to live?'

Million-dollar Question _____

Are you shortening your own life?

Health and fitness are virtually ignored by a preponderance of top executives. High performers at their peak, however, know that every aspect of their lives must be valued. One multimillion-pound company tied executive bonuses to having a yearly medical exam, and some of the top leaders were willing to forgo their bonuses rather than face their own physical conditions.

Wake-up Call

Don't kid yourself about
your health and fitness.

We've all heard the basic rules of peak performers: get the proper amount of rest, eat a good diet and do some exercise. Somehow, many top leaders think they do not need what the rest of us mere mortals must have to be at our best.

Most executives don't pay any attention to the natural rhythms of their bodies. Virtually all those I've worked with drive on relentlessly – irrespective of how their energy levels work. They don't stop and recharge their batteries, despite the fact that they would be far more effective. Something that would have taken ten minutes in the morning might take one hour late at night. Professional athletes are extra-attentive to what works and what doesn't work in terms of driving themselves.

Executives are high performers, too, and should strive to tune in to themselves the way an athlete would, in order to have a work life that would allow them to work at their best.

No athlete would dream of driving hard all the time. They know they would risk burnout. Think about how best to organise yourself so that you have the maximum amount of energy.

Particularly as a leader, how you look counts. If you look exhausted or give off the vibe that your energy is low, your team will pick up on that. Energy is infectious, and everyone around you will benefit from having a more energetic leader.

Stop and Reflect

List the lies you tell yourself or others about your health/ fitness/weight/diet/exercise regimen.

In business, growth is good. In executive waistlines, growth isn't. And, when the company and the CEO's dress size expand at about the same rate, anxiety follows for everyone.

There was too little exercise; there were too many corporate lunches and dinners. And she was leading a healthcare company. Seeing a picture of herself in the local paper accepting an award and looking completely out of shape tipped the scales.

When we first talked, she made the commitment right away to visit the gym twice a week. It was a local gym, and she could fit the visits into her itinerary. But, over the course of three consecutive coaching sessions, she never set one sneakered foot into that gym.

Why? Was she not really committed to the idea? Did the scheduling prove too difficult? Or were there other reasons behind her reluctance? I dug a little deeper.

'I know. I know. I ought to go. But the truth is I hate it. I hate the gym. I hate the idea of communal exercise.'

'Then don't do it,' I told her, sensing her debilitating guilt. 'You don't have to go to the gym. Let's find another way for you to get fit – something you'll enjoy.'

She thought for a moment. 'Well, I used to love bicycling,' she said, then began to hedge. 'But I have to tell you right up front: I'm a little reluctant to buy a bicycle. I've already got a stationary bike at home – and a rowing machine. I don't need to add more machines I won't use. Plus, there's my husband . . .'

'Your husband?'

> **Leadership Note:** *Without your health, you have nothing.*

'Yes, he's a terrific athlete and loves going to that gym. We were supposed to do this together. And he doesn't like cycling.'

'Well, why don't you try it anyway? Let's agree you can go back to the gym idea if the bicycling doesn't work out. But first, maybe you can borrow a bike for a few days instead of buying one. Or even rent one.'

As it turned out, having a 12-year-old son and living in the country with plenty of lightly travelled roads made bicycling a perfect activity. She went out three times that first week and then set a routine for herself that steadily improved her fitness – and greatly increased her time with her son, too. Best of all, her husband bought a bike, and the trio began taking long bicycle excursions together at weekends.

Wake-up Call

Make it graphic.

Generally when I start coaching people I make a distinction between results and well-being: 'Which would you rather have in your work life, outstanding results or outstanding well-being?' Generally people say both; however, they invariably say they feel stressed.

Then we play the well-being game and draw a chart. Under the heading of 'well-being', I ask, 'How would you like your work life to feel?' Typical answers include enjoyable, relaxed, energised.

Draw up three graphs. One for each well-being goal you choose. The vertical axis measures feelings from 0 (worst) to 10 (best), and the horizontal axis lists the days of the week. At the end of each day, plot each of those graphs.

Something very often happens: generally speaking, graphs go up through time. My belief is that by bringing more awareness to how work is feeling, people either consciously or unconsciously make adjustments.

The other thing it enables me to do is to then use the graphs as entry points to coaching around those topics. What was so enjoyable about *that* day, or what was so draining about *that* one? Once they have the graphs, I ask them to give themselves an average over the last three months on a 0–10 scale and to have a goal. It's a way of translating well-being and day-to-day experience into something subjectively quantifiable.

It is not a hard science, but people can get a sense of a productive day versus a frustrating one. This exercise starts to get them much more attentive to productivity rather than just being busy.

Wake-up Call

Be a corporate athlete.

Strive to find some way of keeping fit. Give yourself permission to pursue something you love to do. Gain focus by coming back to the question of this chapter: Would you do anything differently if you knew you had only a year to live? Don't focus only on what's practical. If you don't enjoy the process, it's much less likely that you'll stick to it. If you can't find a physical activity that you enjoy, focus on the outcome rather than the experience itself.

Only the fittest survive, but even the fittest may baulk at an overwhelming challenge. When a company I worked with took over a global sweet manufacturer and launched a three-year roll-out of a new global IT system, the executive they selected to head it up hesitated.

Despite having a handpicked team and the best of everything needed to get the job done – and though he was confident he could deliver the project on time and on budget – he was still worried.

'The demands of this project will probably wreck me physically,' he told me. 'Plus, I expect some of the team members will break down under the stress.'

Implementation of the vast and incredibly complicated system would stretch their abilities to the limit. Travel would be constant, at-home and family time minimal.

We began to look at how he could maintain a fitness regimen throughout the project, and soon decided that fitness and health should be added to the team's objectives. So, not only would they deliver the project as required, they'd be no less healthy and fit in the end than when they started.

He shared his plan: stay only in hotels with pools and workout facilities; schedule no meetings before nine o'clock in the morning at least three days a week; arrange for healthy food choices at all business lunches and dinners; reserve Fridays for catching up and travelling home. Then he told his team what his weight and cholesterol levels were and asked for their support in keeping himself fit.

Finally, he invited them to consider creating their own three-year fitness routines and making personal health one of their objectives during the project.

There were two notable results.

First, the project hit its mark. It was done in less than three years, and all team members remained healthy.

Second, the team member who began the project significantly overweight used the experience as a wake-up call. Like the others, he reaped the financial reward and won kudos for a job well done. But, where they survived with their good health intact, he thrived.

He walked away fitter.

Million-dollar Question

If someone you love died today, what would you regret?

There are three answers I receive most often when I ask the above question:

1. They would regret that they had not communicated how much they loved and cared about the individual.

2. They would regret that they had not paid enough attention to supporting the other person's life. Most of the attention was put on supporting their own career and the loved one's needs were neglected.

3. They would regret that, because of stresses and strain at work, they complained at home. They would go home and 'kick the cat', and moan and groan about work, taking out their stress on their partners and families.

Stop and Reflect

Make an 'I wish' list.

Make a list of things preceded by 'I wish'. Then figure out what's blocking you from turning those wishes into realities. Write down the worst thing you can imagine happening if you had the work–life balance you say you want. Now write down the best thing. Now, how willing are you to play it your way? On a scale of 0–10, rate yourself on bravery.

Here's what an advertising agency's creative director wished for:

1. increased activities with her teenage daughters;

2. more time with her husband;

3. to create a back garden oasis complete with a lap pool to encourage exercise; and

4. more leisure time to reconnect with friends she felt she'd neglected.

She was an incredibly busy woman with a high-demand job to which she was absolutely devoted. She had been successful and was well respected. And she loved her family. 'But', she said, 'I want more in my life than just work and my family.'

Stop and Reflect

If you often find yourself thinking 'If only …', it's time to take back responsibility for your life and your schedule.

So I asked her, 'Can you make one change for each of the items on your wish list in the next six months?'

She said she was willing to try, although she was sceptical about the practicality of adding more to her already full daily life. We talked, she gave it serious thought, and soon she brought me her plan. In the next six months, she would:

1. create a teen haven for her daughter, to encourage her to invite friends over more, and be available for the late-night talks her daughter craved;

2. have a date night scheduled once a week with her husband;

3. hire a garden designer to work with her on creating the back garden paradise she and her family envisioned; and

4. buy a second home in Spain and invite her friends and extended family to visit.

> **Leadership Note:** *Nobody can give you the life you say you want. You have to give yourself permission to create it.*

She achieved all these goals in the six months, and, as we discussed her accomplishments, I asked her, 'So, what have you learned?'

'Oh, that's simple,' she said. 'When it comes to living, it's now or never. There's no "later".'

Putting an imaginary limit on the time you have left is certainly a way of focusing your attention. Let's hope you're never faced with that dilemma, but, if it makes you a better person and a better leader, it's a thought-provoking experiment worth conducting.

Executive Summary

Million-dollar Questions

- Is the ladder you're climbing up leaning against the right wall? What do you really want?

- What kind of role model are you for your employees?

- Are you shortening your own life?

- If someone you love died today, what would you regret?

Stop and Reflect

- Make the most of living life instead of mostly living with regrets.

- The only person who can change the balance in your life is you.

- What would your life partner or your children say was the most important thing in your life?

- List the lies you tell yourself or others about your health/ fitness/weight/diet/exercise regimen.

- Make an 'I wish' list.

- If you often find yourself thinking 'If only . . .', it's time to take back responsibility for your life and your schedule.

Wake-up Calls

- Remember, you're at this point in your family relationships only once – this moment won't come back.

- Be bold and take a risk.

- Don't kid yourself about your health and fitness.

- Make it graphic – draw up charts for your well-being goals.

- Be a corporate athlete.

Leadership Notes

- It helps to remember that you have only one life.

- Without your health, you have nothing.

- Nobody can give you the life you say you want. You have to give yourself permission to create it.

If your people are your biggest asset, why don't they know who you are?

TOM PETERS NAMED 'management by wandering around' as one of the key traits of excellent leaders in his legendary book *In Search of Excellence* (Warner Books, 1982). More than two decades later, I'm amazed at the number of senior managers I coach who don't routinely interact with employees. Indeed, once they are ensconced in the executive offices for the day, they seldom venture out amid the troops. Simply stated, I've observed that few leaders spend sufficient time with their people. They don't know anything about the people they lead and vice versa.

I'm not saying you have to know every employee by name. Obviously, that's impossible in many organisations. I *am* suggesting, however, that you need to make an effort to get to know something about the employees with whom you are in regular contact. Otherwise you'll never know what's really going on in your company. Your employees are not going to open up to a mysterious stranger, and, sadly, that's all many leaders are to the very people who watch over them every day.

Open any annual report, and you're likely to see a glossy tribute extolling the virtues of the corporation's unsung heroes: the employees. Nice sentiment, but in many corporations, that's all it is.

Million-dollar Question

If someone watched you for a week, would they know that your company believes its people are its greatest asset?

Imagine the shock. When they read the staff survey, executives in one of the world's leading high-tech companies discovered they were ineffective leaders. Several respondents noted feeling 'like production units instead of like people' and being treated 'like machines'. Some commented that they joined the company because of its stellar leadership-development record, which they now realised was designed only to help them in dealings with clients and failed to address leadership skills within the organisation.

The senior executives at the top believed in recruiting the brightest and best, prided themselves on career development and affirmed a guiding central principle: 'We develop and nurture.' The staff thought that mission statement should be rewritten: 'Clients first, company second, staff – who?'

Despite their good intentions, what the senior leaders didn't know was how distant they had become. Exclusively focused on clients, they no longer knew their co-workers – other than their immediate team members – at the rapidly growing company. So, rather than risk mistaking a co-worker for a client or vice versa, when sharing an elevator or passing in a corridor, they simply looked away.

Smiling can be easily coached. But changing values and beliefs requires a more potent treatment. In this case, it took name tags. On the pretext of increasing security, name tags were issued. That immediately distinguished the employees from the clients. It also turned employees back into people with names and morale steadily improved.

Million-dollar Question

Are you listening to your people?

For astute leaders, you have only to listen and you'll hear plenty of clues as to what pleases the troops.

Wake-up Call

When closing the staff restaurant was food for thought.

When a large distribution business moved to a swank new head office, management decided to close the staff restaurant and gave employees a slight salary increase so that they could eat out where they pleased. It would be a chance to get out of the office.

The grumbling began almost immediately. As it turned out, the staff restaurant served as a communal centre. People loved being together over lunch. The leadership also failed to realise how much business was done over lunch when people were relaxed.

Because the executive team were out of step with the people, they missed how important a gathering place the restaurant was socially and commercially. The managing director quickly declared that building a new restaurant would be made part of the plan.

Stop and Reflect

Look at the photographs on desks of employees in your immediate area. How many of the stories do you know behind those pictures?

If, on looking at employees' photos, you know very few of the stories behind those pictures, you probably don't know the real story behind the image your company is projecting, either.

Every human being needs to feel important and appreciated. Take note of the connection between a fun, positive atmosphere at work and positive results. Monitor the atmosphere you create. Are people more motivated after spending time with you? Make it a goal never to leave someone less motivated at the end of the conversation than when it started.

Million-dollar Question

Do you treat your internal customers (your employees and suppliers) with as much respect as your external customers?

When I asked the receptionist if I could see the chief executive, she struck up a conversation. 'Did you know our CEO before he started here?' she asked.

'No, as a matter of fact I only met him last month. Why do you ask?'

'Because he seems very pleasant, a truly nice person.'

'That's my impression of him, too. Do you mind telling me why you think he's nice?'

She smiled. 'No, not at all. He's a little different from other executives. He always acknowledges us, says hello. He has a nice smile. You know, the other day on my colleague's birthday, he brought in a cake.'

'That's great! I suppose others feel the same about him?'

'Yes, we all think he's terrific, and we're glad he's in charge. Makes us optimistic. Sure is better than before.'

'How is it better?'

'Well, the last guy, for the whole two years I knew him, never spoke to me. He'd just come through here, show his pass to security, and go on up. I guess he was good at his job. He just wasn't the friendly type.'

Leadership Note: *People don't care how much you know. They want to know how much you care.*

I recounted the conversation to the chief executive moments later.

'Glad to hear that,' he said. 'I like to know that people feel good about themselves and know they're appreciated. In her case, she's got a pretty repetitive job without much glamour. Just think: she has to be charming for eight hours a day – no matter the circumstances. But what a great impression it makes when she's the first person people meet when they visit. So, if she feels good about working here, I think we're doing something right in terms of taking care of our people.'

Wake-up Call

Make yourself a real person to your team.

The bank's new CEO planned a full-auditorium introduction of himself for the first week.

'What are you going to tell them?' I asked him.

'I thought I'd give them a little "delighted to be here", then get into a banking sector review, mergers and acquisition strategy, and a frank assessment of our position relative to invasive competitors.'

'Sounds revolutionary,' I teased. I had coached him before and felt free to challenge him. 'You know, you might think about your tone. What do you want people to take away from that first meeting?'

'Naturally, I hope they get a sense of my view of the business. They should see my leadership style. And I'd like them to experience what kind of person I am.'

'Does any of that come across in the introduction you described?'

'It was a little heavy on the business end, wasn't it?'

We talked through how he might do it differently and crafted the plan.

He ditched the banker's dark suit and tie and strolled on stage in slacks and shirt. 'I'm thrilled to be here,' he said, and, as a Power-Point presentation lit up the giant screen behind him, he began to talk about himself, his early years and his family. A picture of his wife appeared, then his son. Then there was another image of him, muddy and looking silly, surrounded by his 10-year-old's rugby team.

'I wanted you to know that there are more passions in my life than just banking,' he said. 'I'm sure you have many passions, too. It's what makes us interesting – and human.'

His medium was his message. He modelled the ethos he envisioned for the business.

When he moved into his views on the banking sector, it was succinct, pointed and interspersed with cartoons. Then he stopped for questions.

Stop and Reflect

Can you create an atmosphere where people feel free to ask questions?

Because we knew people would be hesitant to ask about the burning issues on everyone's mind, we had a few people in the audience ask some tough ones to ease the natural anxiety: 'What's your management style? Slash and burn?' and 'How long are you planning to stay?' and 'How do you feel about redundancies?' That helped establish an ask-anything atmosphere and give voice to what many probably wondered.

He concluded with a promise to listen to their feedback and suggestions and to lead as effectively as he knew how. They responded with thunderous applause.

Stop and Reflect

Find a way to see beyond what your team *want* you to see.

After his first three months, the new CEO wanted a more direct experience of the business. He decided to work in the company's factory for a week.

He asked me what I thought. 'It's brilliant,' I said. 'What do they think at the factory?'

'They're already starting to scrub and shine.'

But that would spoil what he wanted: the true experience of factory work. So we set up a series of lunches at the canteen, informal chats with his soon-to-be co-workers, and he put them at ease by talking through his expectation of no special treatment.

An idea appeared. We could get more mileage from the process if he penned a 'Dear Diary' column about his experience for the company magazine.

Then the factory workers decided that one from their ranks should shadow the CEO in his executive role for a week and write a column of his own.

Stop and Reflect

Put yourself in the shoes of each person you lead.

It became a cultural exchange programme, with an entire edition of the company magazine devoted to the blue-collar view of the boardroom and executive observations on factory life. There were photographs, too – the CEO looking oddly well groomed in overalls and hard hat, the factory worker dressed up in his good suit.

Bridges of understanding were built between disparate branches of the company as the accounts of the adventures were shared. And a trade journal later picked up the story.

> **Leadership Note:** *Walk the talk. Leaders need to be seen.*

These days executives dart about from company to company and have rarely done the jobs of the people they are commissioned to lead. You cannot lead from an ivory tower.

A CEO of a top retailer took his team on a field trip through the stores. Along the way, they discussed Christmas displays. The staff appreciated the interest.

Time spent with employees and with customers is undervalued. You cannot find out what's really going on by presentations and reports.

Wake-up Call

Cultivate a genuine interest in your staff.

Another chief executive I coached some years ago didn't believe in *management by walking around* (MBWA). 'I hate small talk,' he said. Frankly, nobody wanted to talk to him, either. He was severe and challenging. He scared people away. And chasing them down with winsome banter proved too difficult.

His only relationships were among the investors, where his strategic thinking earned him respect. But, as a people person, he earned the nickname 'the Grim Reaper'.

'Did you know they called you that?' I asked him.

He actually laughed out loud. 'I probably come across like him.'

Stop and Reflect _____

Learn to make small talk or you'll miss important clues to making the business better.

He asked how he could learn to make small talk and turn attitudes around. We created a plan that had him strolling the maze of cubicles and asking simple questions about the personalisation he observed there: 'Is that a picture of your wife?' 'Hey, that's a great cartoon. Where'd you find it?' 'Is that a bowling trophy?'

It's easy for people to talk about what they find meaningful, and he could listen. As he relaxed and they became more comfortable, he asked, 'If I had my magic CEO wand with me, what's the number-one thing you'd want me to magically fix?'

People heard his question as a potent one because it meant the CEO was eager to listen and address problems.

Million-dollar Question

When is the last time you walked around and talked to your employees?

At the regular offsite meetings, he asked team members to bring symbols of their work and personal lives, drew them into games of gentle, playful disclosure, and joined them in the sharing of stories and dreams.

He got to know them, and they got to know him.

Stop and Reflect

The next time you are with an employee, ask this question: What's your biggest problem? Listen closely to the answer and take action on what is divulged.

Wake-up Call

Don't make your secretaries unhappy.

The relocated office building was more convenient, modern, and had more amenities. But the secretaries were grumbling. Leave it to the coach to ask why.

It was the printers.

In the old office, every secretary had a printer. In the new office, centralised – 'more efficient' – print centres dotted the floor plan at strategic intervals, and the secretaries' print jobs were getting jammed in behind PowerPoint printouts, multiple copies of big reports, and downloaded PDFs.

Make a secretary wait and unhappiness will spread. Secretaries got their printers back, and their smiles returned.

Million-dollar Question

Are you fun to be around? Hint: if you cringe at the thought, you probably aren't.

They called him 'the drone' behind his back, because he wasn't much fun. In fact, he didn't even like the word fun. He asked me to say 'enjoyment' instead of 'fun', which he thought sounded too flippant.

We discussed the relationship between enjoyment and productivity, management and morale, laughter and stress. He was willing to take small steps.

At the monthly, offsite team meeting, he pushed the conference table to a corner and circled the chairs. He slipped off his jacket and tie and cranked up music during breaks.

Stop and Reflect

What adjectives would an outsider use to describe the people you lead? The meetings you run? Your leadership style? Rate the morale and sense of fun in your area of responsibility on a scale of 0–10.

After three months, the team reported more openness and energy. He was ready for another little step towards enjoyment.

He blocked out agenda time for casual conversations and challenged the tyranny of endless PowerPoint presentations. At the office, Friday became dress-down day; meeting rooms had décor makeovers with more comfortable chairs, art on the walls, and music piped in. A daily joke was posted.

Eventually, the dress code was relaxed to casual five days a week, unless clients came. And, as retention rates rose and the air of openness prevailed, it was clear 'Darth' had returned from his stint on the dark side.

> **Leadership Note:** *Sustained high performance comes when you are satisfied and enjoying life. Your positive outlook energises those around you.*

Wake-up Call

It's important to know what your people need from you.

I hired a young man as my COO. During his six-month review, he said, 'You're not supporting me.' I thought, That's exactly what a coach doesn't want to hear.

Naturally, I assumed that this executive – I'd known him for years and coached him through incredible growth experiences – was telling me he needed more one-on-one meetings, more input, more ideas. So that's what I gave him. And, when I checked in at six months, I expected to hear 'problem solved, good job'.

Instead, I got another slap in the face. He was 'disappointed' that 'nothing has changed'.

Flabbergasted, and trying hard not to be defensive, I reviewed the coaching sessions, the key topics and the problem solving of the recent months. Where did he see a lack of support?

'Wait a minute,' he said. 'That's not what I meant.'

'Then tell me what you meant, would you?'

'I need you to support my position. We need to agree before a meeting, then present a united front on a subject under discussion. Instead, you're challenging me in meetings. That doesn't help me, and it's not good for the process.'

I breathed a sigh of relief. I wasn't stupid, I had just misunderstood. And misunderstanding can be fixed so much more easily than incompetence.

Sometimes words have different meanings to different people. Often in a group, someone will say, 'We need more communication in this business.' Don't jump to a conclusion about what that statement means. If you go around the conference table, you'll likely hear 10 different versions of what 'more communication' means. This encounter with my own employee was a wonderful example of how two experts in the field of communication don't always get it right.

Leadership Note: *Practise what you preach.*

Performance equals potential minus interference. Eliminate 'us and them' silo behaviour – in other words, behaviour that focuses on just your area without thinking about how your role fits into the organisation as a whole. Keep your antennae up all the time. Don't underestimate the importance of your internal customers. If one fails, we all fail. Communicate, communicate and communicate with your employees and suppliers.

Million-dollar Question

Are you willing to tackle the tough issues? Or do you turn a blind eye?

Wake-up Call

Addressing an issue head-on
is often the best policy.

Two pharmaceutical companies merged. There were meetings for strategising. There was a team-building adventure.

There was one man's notable drinking to excess. In fact, after several stiff drinks at the party the night before, he failed to show for the morning meeting.

The new CEO was shocked that people seemed willing to pass it off as the norm with this man. We discussed a few possible avenues. The CEO consulted with the head of human resources. The CEO could confront the situation or turn it over. But he couldn't ignore what had become both a human and a business problem. Morale suffered, with co-workers gingerly skirting the situation. And operations felt the effects of missed meetings, tardiness and dropped projects.

He decided to address the issue head-on and called the man in.

'I'm concerned for you,' he said. He made it clear that his drinking problem wouldn't be tolerated and offered to send him to a rehab centre. The man accepted the offer and eventually rejoined the company as a solid contributor.

Stop and Reflect

Every team member is important. You cannot afford to ignore problems.

During one quarter, the phone bill at my company was off the map. Somebody from the secretarial area was making calls several times a day to a premium-rate astrology line. I spoke to the woman who was in charge of the secretaries. We agreed to make an announcement about the problem. We requested the person come forward privately, or we would be forced to monitor calls. A woman confessed to the unfortunate conduct, and we dealt with the problem in a way that maintained her dignity and her job.

> **Leadership Note:** *Your staff really are your greatest asset, and every team member deserves to be treated with dignity and respect. Believe it, and you'll tackle the tough stuff with ease.*

Wake-up Call

Corporate culture needs a little more love.

Long before it was fashionable to see a company's people and culture as key assets, I worked with a group of executives from a FTSE 100 firm on a novel approach to workforce management. It was a little touchy-feely for the time, but their interest was high.

During lunch, someone asked my colleague, 'What would make the biggest difference in performance when managing people?'

He quickly answered, 'There needs to be more love in the workplace.'

The room fell utterly, dreadfully silent. Apparently, they could handle innovative management skills, but they weren't ready for love. I salvaged the rest of the event the best I could, but their enthusiasm was gone. Reviews were middling, and I was later taken aside.

'We may bring you back for further discussion of your management programme, but under no circumstances is your colleague to be involved with us again.' The person went on to tell me that the company viewed my colleague's comments as inappropriate and unprofessional.

Twenty-five years later, we haven't made that much progress in corporate culture.

Million-dollar Question

Do people know you appreciate them?

Wake-up Call

Say 'thank you' and you'll say so much more.

One chief information officer charged her personal assistant with sending thank-you emails to staff members. The assistant watched for special individual efforts, then composed messages and dispatched them from the executive's email address.

It worked reasonably well until someone caught on. They weren't genuine communiqués from the boss: they were templates. And, even though the executive genuinely intended to recognise individual efforts, her attempt to make it easier on herself back-fired.

'How does this get done in other businesses?' she asked me.

'The best of them send handwritten notes to their employees' homes. It takes time, but it's infinitely more personal.'

Stop and Reflect

Catch people doing things right. List one thing for which they would each like to be positively acknowledged.

She weighed the effects of continuing her gratitude-by-proxy programme or switching to something more direct. 'I don't know how I'll find time to actually write to each employee,' she said.

But, when she did, many of the notes were framed and hung on cubicle and office walls.

Wake-up Call

**Get your people involved – and
they'll get to know you better.**

A new product development director had the glamorous part: travelling first class, visiting five continents, and looking for ideas to spawn nifty new electronics and gadgets.

Back in the United States, his team managed the support side and contended with suppliers, factories and marketing departments. They admired him, but rumbled with discontent as he jetted around the planet while they learned nothing about how he picked up on trends that translated into new products.

Leadership Note: *It's time to nip negativity in the bud.*

We talked about what he could do. He wanted to convince his team members that they were valued and that he was committed to their development. He hoped to challenge their perception of his role as glamorous. And he needed to take meaningful action.

So he told his team that he understood what it was like to have the back-at-the-ranch job and passionately re-emphasised how critical they were to the process. 'I also understand that I haven't helped any of you develop your own new product design abilities. I'm sorry and want to change that.'

He explained that much of his work was wearisome – living out of a suitcase, working across language and custom barriers for last-minute deals, coping with flight delays and airport terminals.

'Nevertheless, I think you should join me. And that's why I'll make no more trips alone – one of you will always come with me.

I expect you to share with your colleagues when you return, educating each other about your experiences. Together, we'll make all of you into great new-product geniuses!'

His surprising announcement was followed by a more surprising action. From that point forward, he returned from each of his trips with a hand-selected gift for each team member. He used the gifts as talking points in instructive discussions about new products and trends.

His thoughtful plan completely reversed the discontent. It also went a long way to helping his people to get to know him better, instead of wondering half the time who and where he was!

> **Leadership Note:** *Success depends on collaboration and unity.*

Wake-up Call

**Squash parochial behaviour.
Write a one-sentence statement
naming actions that won't be tolerated.**

One of the key findings that emerged from the Chicago, Illinois-based Hudson Highland Centre for High Performance's global study on high-performing business units was that high-performing individuals talk about and think about things that are related to the performance of that business unit in a positive sense. They don't think and talk about things that are negative.

Sometimes I ask people I coach to tell me what they think is being talked about during casual contact in the business – in corridors, cars, taxis, lifts, or when people brush up against each other. 'Tell me what you think is on people's minds,' I urge.

Some mention day-to-day expressions of various parts of the culture. Others describe negative comments on the direction of the company or the leadership or a certain part of the business. Sometimes the IT department is cast in the role of the villain. Sometimes it's Human Resources or Marketing. In retailing, it's often the stores or distribution centres or the head office that are the 'bad guys'. A common theme is blame: 'We did our part; if only they'd done theirs.'

Stop and Reflect

Kill gossip. Quantify the toll that rumours took on your business during the past month.

If the person I'm coaching speculates that those negative conversations are going on, I ask them what that's doing for the business. Negativity creates pictures of the business that aren't necessarily accurate, yet they become solidified and hardwired as a belief within the organisation. Obviously, it's not doing the business any good when adversarial or distanced relationships pop up in the organisation.

'Put a financial figure on the lack of partnership and collaboration,' I'll say. Of course, they can't come up with a hard number on the cost to the company. I just ask the question to get people to recognise that this behaviour has a significant negative impact. Lay some ground rules to squash negativity. Everyone from the board downwards must abide by those rules.

> **Leadership Note:** *Whenever you have a grievance, take it only to somebody who can fix it. Have conversations only with people who can affect things positively.*

Wake-up Call

**Look after the people who
look after the customers.**

The new CEO of the troubled online and catalogue retailer was surprised to learn that customers were on the bottom of the list of priorities, and a close second were the customer service workers. The lavish executive offices were in stark contrast to the dark and dingy offices where the masses servicing the customers slaved away fielding phone calls and irate emails from customers.

He made changes. 'First,' he said, 'after the customers, the most important people are the people serving customers.'

Then he renamed the head office the 'customer support centre' and decreed that two days a month everyone would work either on the phone or on computers fielding customer complaints and enquiries.

This upset the senior executives because they didn't like being forced to demonstrate how little they knew about what went on with the customers. By comparison, life at the executive suites had been sweet indeed.

Just as the senior executives were getting over being upset about the mandatory monthly bumbling-around-not-knowing-what-they-were-doing time dealing with customers, the CEO posted a schedule for board meetings – to be held in the company break rooms instead of the beautifully appointed boardroom on the top floor. Employees were invited. Some were even asked to report.

The CEO rolled out a process that clarified the relationship of each person to the customers. When a person's role didn't connect in an obvious way to the needs of the customer, the CEO had questions about exactly what that person's contributions to the company were.

Then, for the four weeks leading up to Christmas, the CEO declared that everybody in the support office would be working the phone lines and computers, with a skeleton crew in operations. 'Whatever we were doing before is not as important as our customers,' he said. Again, his actions backed up what he said mattered: the people who served the customers.

Not surprisingly, the people who had mattered most *before* the new CEO took over weren't especially pleased with the new CEO.

On the other hand, the people who had mattered the least – customers and employees who served them – were very happy about the ways the stores had changed. And that turned the troubled retailer around.

Executive Summary

Million-dollar Questions

- If someone watched you for a week, would they know that your company believes its people are its greatest asset?

- Are you listening to your people?

- Do you treat your internal customers (your employees and suppliers) with as much respect as your external customers?

- When is the last time you walked around and talked to your employees?

- Are you fun to be around? Hint: if you cringe at the thought, you probably aren't.

- Are you willing to tackle the tough issues? Or do you turn a blind eye?

- Do people know you appreciate them?

Stop and Reflect

- Look at the photographs on desks of employees in your immediate area. How many of the stories do you know behind those pictures?

- Can you create an atmosphere where people feel free to ask questions?

- Find a way to see beyond what your team *want* you to see.

- Put yourself in the shoes of each person you lead.

- Learn to make small talk or you'll miss important clues to making the business better.

- The next time you are with an employee, ask this question: What's your biggest problem? Listen closely to the answer and take action on what is divulged.

- What adjectives would an outsider use to describe the people you lead? The meetings you run? Your leadership style? Rate the morale and sense of fun in your area of responsibility on a scale of 0–10.

- Every team member is important. You cannot afford to ignore problems.

- Catch people doing things right. List one thing for which they would each like to be positively acknowledged.

- Kill gossip. Quantify the toll that rumours took on your business during the past month.

Wake-up Calls

- When closing the staff restaurant was food for thought – and reopening it brought employees together again.

- Make yourself a real person to your team.

- Cultivate a genuine interest in your staff.

- Don't make your secretaries unhappy.

- It's important to know what your people need from you.

- Addressing an issue head-on is often the best policy.

- Corporate culture needs a little more love.

- Say 'thank you' and you'll say so much more.

- Get your people involved – and they'll get to know you better.

- Squash parochial behaviour. Write a one-sentence statement naming actions that won't be tolerated.

- Look after the people who look after the customers.

Leadership Notes

- People don't care how much you know. They want to know how much you care.

- Walk the talk. Leaders need to be seen.

- Sustained high performance comes when you are satisfied and enjoying life. Your positive outlook energises those around you.

- Practise what you preach.

- Your staff really are your greatest asset, and every team member deserves to be treated with dignity and respect. Believe it, and you'll tackle the tough stuff with ease.

- It's time to nip negativity in the bud.

- Success depends on collaboration and unity.

- Whenever you have a grievance, take it only to somebody who can fix it. Have conversations only with people who can affect things positively.

Who pays your salary and why are you ignoring them?

FEW LEADERS PAY ENOUGH ATTENTION to their customers and clients. How do you know whether *you* do – or don't? How much of your information about customers comes from focus groups and third-party surveys? If more than half your knowledge about customers comes from outside sources, you've lost touch with people who are critical to your company's survival and to your continued success.

I don't recommend that you become a micromanager and frustrate your employees. But, periodically, you must come down from the mountaintop and walk on ground level among the people who buy and use your products and services. You've got to be shoulder to shoulder with your customers when you look at the competition, too. And you can't let somebody else do it for you. A good leader relies on intuition and an understanding of the nuances of consumers' buying decisions – and you can get that only from being where the action is.

How do customers feel about your brand and how do they feel

about the contact they have with your people? Do you know how people who buy your services or your product view your company?

We all know the numbers that show it's more economical and easier on resources to keep a customer than get a new one. Knowing that fact intellectually is one thing. Deciding to lead in a way that makes certain your company retains or gains the *wow!* factor – something that makes your company attractive for customers – is another altogether.

The best way to realise what your customers are experiencing is to become one or to work in a part of the business where you'll be close to them. Work in the call centre, work in the stores, or shop in your own place.

I've recommended this in my coaching many times over the years, but my suggestion usually meets resistance. Leaders are fearful of getting out there and confronting reality. They're far more comfortable with what gets filtered up through the organisation to their desks.

One of my clients decreed that once a month the whole executive team would work in a different part of the business. Over a 12-month period, the team would see every part of the business. And guess what. Once that practice was implemented, the company's customer satisfaction numbers took a big jump.

Million-dollar Question

What adjectives would describe your experience with your company? What do your customers want or need that isn't being addressed? What could be done better, faster or cheaper?

Wake-up Call

Put yourself in your customers' shoes.

If you are not known around the business, pose as a customer and see what the experience is like. Go unannounced. And, while you're out there, take a look at the competition. Ask yourself, What are we better at, and what are we worse at? That sort of in-the-trenches experience gives you data that doesn't emerge from focus groups, and it's far more compelling than anything you'll learn from charts, spreadsheets, and reports.

One manufacturer and marketer of a major consumer product directed the executive team to spend time shopping in retail stores as part of their quarterly board meeting. The team split up and went to different parts of the country. In the stores, the executives were not allowed to ask for their company's brand. Instead, they had to purchase whatever the sales assistant recommended. Upon reconvening, the executives reported on the competition and on what they learned from the shopping experience.

Leadership Note: *Make sure you get the picture.*

One CEO of a large discount retail chain was exasperated after an experience in one of his own stores. He bought a few small items and was surprised when the sales assistant unceremoniously dumped them in his hands. 'May I have a bag?' he asked.

'We don't give out plastic bags for purchases under five pounds,' said the assistant.

'You're kidding me.'

'No, sir. But I can sell you one for twenty pence.'

The CEO was incredulous. As it turns out, several of the cashiers had complained that the policy was costing the chain customers, but their complaints were falling on deaf ears. However, after his 'handful of experience', the CEO immediately scrapped the policy. Who knows, however, how many customers were lost while the company tried to save on plastic bags?

At another company, the CEO liked the idea of getting out to the stores and interacting with frontline people. He scheduled the visits months in advance.

'I bet you see a lot of tidiness,' I said. When you know the king's coming, you put out clean towels.

'You bet. We've got great people out there doing marvellous work. Everywhere I go it looks terrific.'

'What do you think happens when a store manager knows you're coming?'

He said somewhat sheepishly, 'I suppose they scramble to make sure the stockroom is tidy and the shelves are fully stocked.'

'I'm sure that's what happens. So what you see is what they *want* you to see during the royal visit versus what customers experience when they shop. What if you dropped in unannounced?'

He thought for a moment. 'I suppose I'd see what our customers see.'

In fact, what he subsequently discovered was that store managers actually lent staff to each other when they knew the CEO was coming. It was a legacy from the previous CEO whose autocratic style had employees shaking in their boots. The new CEO wasn't getting a true picture until he began dropping in unannounced.

That's when he found what customers routinely encountered: empty shelves. The inaccurate information that his predecessor had relied upon based on the royal visits had led to an unwieldy supply chain. Now the CEO knew what he was dealing with and could get down to business.

Leadership Note: *Treat your customers like royalty.*

Wake-up Call

Take a good look in the mirror.
Remember that customer service starts
at the top. A dose of your own medicine
might be bitter, but it can also start to
cure what's ailing in your organisation.

The executives had a long agenda in mind for their meeting with their advertising agency. They made their way to the usual reception room and found it littered with rubbish. No one was there.

A receptionist appeared. She didn't know who they were or anything about a meeting. 'How did you get past security?' she asked.

She rang several phone extensions before she found someone who could help. 'Boardroom. Third floor. Second door on the right.' She didn't smile.

There was no one waiting for them in that room, either, although it appeared someone had been there recently. Dirty cups, pizza boxes, and half-eaten sandwiches were strewn about. Chairs were askew. Sheets of newsprint with indecipherable scribbles were taped to the walls.

Stop and Reflect

What message are you delivering to your customers on a daily basis?

Incensed, the CEO grabbed the phone to ring the ad agency's boss. That was when the advertising team, led by the boss, entered the room. 'Right now, you feel like your customers,' he said. 'Take a look at this.' He flicked on the video player, and the executives watched footage of customers on their own untidy premises encountering discourteous, ill-prepared staff.

'We can do wonderful things for you,' the ad agency president said. 'But you've got to take care of your business first.'

That story delivers a powerful one-two punch and has made the rounds with consultants. I often wonder how many companies would benefit from a similar wake-up call.

Million-dollar Question

Are your customers thrilled?

Wake-up Call

Check your daily agenda for the percentage of time you spend with customers.

Searching for the source of the bank's trouble, the CEO opened her files on customer complaints. She found neat, monthly reports of call volume.

Nothing about the content.

She also found standard letters that were sent out as a routine reply. 'If they hadn't responded at all, it would have been better than that,' she fumed. Overnight, she changed everything in regard to how customer complaints were handled. First, she renamed the Customer Complaint Department the Customer Service Department. Next, she directed the department to route all complaints to her.

Then she wrote a letter to every customer who had written a letter of complaint. She emailed every customer who emailed a complaint, and she followed up her email with a letter.

Stop and Reflect

Can you remember the last time you spoke with a customer? If not, you're out of touch.

And to every customer who had phoned in a complaint, she sent a letter – although sometimes, when it seemed like the right thing to do, she just picked up the phone and called the irate customer.

Over the next several months, she responded to each complaint personally, and the bank, which had thousands of employees, gradually turned into a customer-focused business. Eventually, she reduced her hands-on involvement and delegated the rapidly shrinking complaint-management task to a personal assistant. She sent the responses with the characteristic flair of the CEO's office and kept her apprised in detail.

Million-dollar Question _____

What does your response to problems say to your customers?

Wake-up Call

How you handle customer service
sends a powerful message about
what matters to you.

At the Alexander Corporation, we tracked our clients' satisfaction. We asked them how they felt about everything from our programmes to our receptionist. And we adapted, based on the feedback we received.

At some point, it occurred to me that we were customers too. And while we did a good job of collecting opinions from our clients, we rarely heard a word from our suppliers. No one phoned me and asked about my experience with their company – not the restaurant we had used 50 times to cater events in the course of a year, not the taxi service, not the hotels.

That started me thinking. If I wasn't hearing from any of those suppliers, I bet my clients weren't hearing much from anyone, either. I decided to spend some time face to face at the end of each yearly meeting with my clients – on a no-fee basis, of course – just to say 'thank you' and ask how we were doing as a company. These were not sales calls.

I'd meet with the CEO or the human-resources director, and my visits were well received. I learned all kinds of ways we could make our service even better.

One thing they told us that they liked was that they got the strong sense that we practised what we preached – a non-hierarchical, open culture. We were role models of team building, unlike many of our competitors.

Second, they noted that, while almost all consultancies claim to tailor work to their clients, their experience showed them that we truly fulfilled that promise. We did not offer off-the-shelf solutions, but listened to their unique problems and designed programmes accordingly.

These two perceptions were important, because they were the key to our competitive edge.

I also discovered some negatives. One of the things clients sought from consultants was a quick response, and our response times often lagged. They understood that we had other clients, but they often felt that we were slow to respond. They questioned whether their business was important to us. They also told us that they didn't like our detail-deficient invoices.

We changed the way we responded to our customers' calls and redesigned our invoices, too. And in the process we learned that when we thanked the companies who worked with us, and offered to make the working relationship even better, it paid an un-expected dividend: they asked for our help with their new projects and referred more new clients to us.

Wake-up Call

Keep your antennae up.

Interestingly enough, people in support functions don't always think of themselves as having customers. Yet, employees and leaders in information technology and human resources or any of the core support or back-office functions all have customers.

When I work with either the leader of one of those functions or a team, I ask, 'Who are your customers?' In many cases they hadn't really thought about the other divisions of the company in that way. I follow up with a second question: 'If they are your customers, what does the customer want and are you delivering it?'

Million-dollar Question

Do you know who your customers are?

The response is often that not only were they clueless in regard to what the needs were, but they had no earthly idea what those departments did. This lack of awareness about how their functions play into the overall picture means that most support functions take a product-led approach, instead of learning what their internal customers want and delivering it.

For example, the HR department will come up with a new annual appraisal scheme for staff and then try to implement it into the business; or the IT department will introduce the latest hot new sales-contact system when the old one was efficient and popular with the salespeople. Your technology people may be turned on by the latest technology and software – whether it meets a business need or not.

Leadership Note: *Everybody in the organisation has a customer.*

A more sensible approach is to find out what your internal customers actually want that enables them to work together more effectively. To make this approach come alive in your company, you may need to facilitate meetings between departments so that they can begin to understand each other. I realise that this sounds obvious, but dialogue between key functions is frequently absent in the corporate world.

For instance, a global transportation company added a new $4 billion IT system. After implementation, however, the consensus was that the service was worse. Why? Because the IT people didn't fully communicate with their internal customers, and the new system was off target. Without asking questions, there is no understanding.

Stop and Reflect —————————————————

Don't underestimate the importance of your internal customers.

Wake-up Call

Eliminate 'us and them' silo thinking.

Positive feedback from customers made the consultancy's management happy. But the good reviews stood out in distinct contrast with the marks internal staff gave the company.

The partners turned their attention to the disparity. They were clear about why the clients were pleased. 'We listen, then deliver what they need. They trust us. They refer other clients to us.'

'Feeling listened to, having their needs met, trusting, referring new business – so, which of those things do you think is inappropriate for your staff?' I asked.

What should clients get that staff do not? And why?

The strictly business approach of the partners was good for clients and great for the company's growth, but internal dissatisfaction gnawed away at the overall sense of success. When the partners turned their skills towards internal staff – listening, meeting needs, winning trust – it made all the difference, measurably reflected in soaring retention rates.

Wake-up Call

Listen to your employees' advice.

A CEO was pawing through the stack of costly, complicated programme proposals, looking for a solution to his customer-service troubles.

'Why not ask the people who work in the stores?' I wondered aloud.

'They're mostly part-timers. Not likely they'll grasp the big picture.'

'You might be underestimating them. You might save a few thousand pounds with a penny for their thoughts.'

'What do you propose?'

'Give me a crack at one of your stores, and we'll see if your employees have any good ideas.'

Just by setting up my session at the store, the CEO was already sending a message: he was willing to take a closer look, try something different, find a solution to persistent problems.

I sat the employees in a circle and asked them to tell me about precious people in their lives. They named partners, children and parents. Then I had them imagine a conversation. 'Your precious person has just come home from a wonderful shopping experience at your store. What happened that made it so wonderful?'

Stop and Reflect

What would make doing business with your company an unforgettable experience?

For a tidy sum – in fact the CEO had received a proposal for a £1 million analysis of his customer service – consultants could have conceived the very list that this roomful of part-time employees generated: friendly and helpful staff, a sparkling clean store, attractive merchandise displays and easy-to-find products. Imagine a good retail shopping experience, and most people think the same way.

It was the manager who asked them, 'What can we do here to help customers have experiences like that – and do you want to?'

Stop and Reflect

Do not try to *guess* what your customer wants.

Absolutely! Happier customers would mean better working conditions all around. The employees prioritised lists and signed up for individual responsibilities.

Armed with their ideas and backed by their commitments, the manager approached the CEO. 'My people would like to make these changes,' he said, and handed him the list of action items. 'We think we can improve how our customers feel about our store, and we're ready to get started, unless you say no.'

Million-dollar Question

Do you really know who your customer is?

Over the next two years, each of the 1,200 stores in the chain ran its own internal planning process, following the example of the first one, and launched self-improvement programmes. Across the company, customer-service ratings improved, store foot traffic and average customer spending increased and employee retention rates rose.

'Those people we've got out there in our stores,' the CEO told me, 'they really know what they're doing.'

Wake-up Call

Get into your customers' lives.

Focus groups and research reports told a retail executive about youth buying trends. 'How do we get you inside the skin of your target market?' I asked. We set up an experiment.

We assigned the executives the profiles of make-believe 18- to 25-year-olds and asked them to describe their interests, leisure time activities and buying habits. We also placed a variety of the company's products on the table so they could talk about their preferences. 'Which do you buy?' 'How often?'

Embarrassment and laughter ensued as the executives revealed how little they knew about youth culture and, in some cases, how little experience they had with the company's products.

When they'd all had their turn, the door opened, and in walked the group of young people whose profiles had been the basis of the exercise.

Their answers to the same questions about lifestyle and spending were startlingly different from the executives' answers. This disclosure convinced the executives they had been off target and triggered new thinking. 'Instead of making products we hope young people will buy, why not get to know the people in the market and offer products we know they want?'

After sharing a meal at a nearby restaurant, the CEO recruited several of the students as regular reality-check consultants.

Leadership Note: *The right products and services, the right place and time, and the right price – these are the keys to customer satisfaction.*

Wake-up Call

Take every opportunity to make the customer's experience with your product come to life.

In my work I've attended many training sessions for companies. At some, products were invisible; at the best-run sessions, the client's products were omnipresent. Now, whenever we run a training session, we insist that our client's products be used wherever possible.

For example, at a hotel during a three-day session, each guest room was stocked with the company's consumer products. With a food retailer we made sure that the meals were made with that particular client's products. At another conference, the chef prepared breakfast, lunch and dinner menus strictly from recipes in the grocery retailer magazine. Executives had a direct experience of what they were putting out for customers. They were pleasantly surprised by how great the food was.

> **Stop and Reflect**
>
> How many customer-service and customer-satisfaction agenda items have you reviewed in the last six months?

Wake-up Call

Don't let your company get sidetracked – its business is its business.

It's all too easy in business to focus on the wrong things. Executives get caught up in reorganising or restructuring, forgetting the point of what the company does.

Every part of one retail business was under scrutiny by overlapping analytical projects that dragged on and on until the new CEO had had enough.

'Stop!' he said. 'No more projects!'

His managers were taken aback. 'No more projects? Then what will we do all day?'

He answered by asking them to name the two most important parts of their retail business. 'Here's a hint,' he said. 'Neither one is a project.'

After thinking it over, they said, 'Supply chain and customer service.'

'Then that's what you should be doing: making the supply chain seamless and making sure our customers get the best service.'

He added, 'So let's decide a reasonable number of projects to have live at one time.'

'Fifty,' a manager suggested.

'Forty? Forty is better,' said another.

'How about six?' asked the CEO. There was a pause.

'Six is good,' they said.

'And we're adding two rules,' announced the CEO. 'First, from now on, every project has to have a due date and must be completed by that date. Second, nobody can start a new project until an old one is finished.' Silence. Then nods all around.

And that's how a new CEO returned the retail business to the business of retail.

Million-dollar Question

How does the change affect the end customer?

I always like to check the values when I go into a new company: What's driving the business? Any mission statement or annual report should express the idea of customer service and the value of a company's own people. Without happy customers, it won't be long until you're out of business.

Wake-up Call

If anyone fails, we all fail.

Another company took a novel approach with its suppliers. It created a sports team out of senior managers and then arranged sporting days with suppliers. Afterwards, the groups sat down to a meal together and talked about quality. That strategy helped the company tap into supplier satisfaction in a new way.

Million-dollar Question _____

Are your suppliers friends or foes?

Wake-up Call

**Communicate, communicate
and communicate with your
employees and suppliers.**

The business was cutthroat, with competitors fighting for best materials, production schedules and delivery times. One company even positioned itself as an adversary of its suppliers. 'They're screwing us with prices and cheating us out of time.'

How did I know this? I read the writing on the wall. At the company's head office, a chart publicly posted in the waiting area showed the five top suppliers of the month and – I couldn't believe what I was seeing – the *five worst* suppliers of the month.

I approached the CEO: 'I'm not sure displaying that information regarding your suppliers is a good idea. First of all, do you want everybody to know who your suppliers are, and, second, how do you think your suppliers feel when they walk in and see their names emblazoned under the heading "worst"?'

Stop and Reflect _____

Are your suppliers your friends or your enemies?

The management team subscribed to the classic view that the supplier relationship was bound to be adversarial. The majority thought the way to get the most was to demand more for less. A minority thought the relationship would be better served if the suppliers were treated more as partners.

'Imagine what it's like to be a supplier with this company,' I urged. Slowly, everyone in the room admitted that suppliers might get more stubborn, because they were being pushed too hard.

Eventually, the CEO said, 'Maybe this isn't the cleverest way to play suppliers.'

With tensions high and little hope of resolution, I had another question: 'Have you ever talked?'

Both sides agreed to a workshop to discuss the relationship. At first, we kept them in separate rooms, working on flipcharts: how we see ourselves, how we see them, how we think they see us.

I hid the sharp objects and called them together. 'The rules are simple,' I said. 'First, be honest and fair. Second, remember that the aim is an effective, professional relationship, not necessarily love.'

As the disclosure unfolded, it was the company that faced the greater challenges. Its rigidity about deadlines had forced deliveries to be late. Even when the suppliers saw delays coming – due to weather, international incidents and factory fires – they'd learned there was no point pleading for extensions. And the company missed an opportunity for collaborative problem solving. The suppliers, defeated by the lack of dialogue, routinely missed the deadlines and took the criticism on the chin.

Leadership Note: *Problem solving is a collaborative exercise.*

At the same time, when they listened to the company's side of the story, the suppliers came to a new understanding of their role with the company. Where they had often felt used, they now felt relied on.

Tension dissipated, and the conversation turned to plans for continuing dialogue and strengthening of the relationships.

Back at the company headquarters, the posting of best and worst monthly suppliers that had hung behind the receptionist's desk was replaced with pictures of the company's customers.

So why have we moved from the question posed in the title of this chapter to discuss your relationship with suppliers? While it's true that customers ultimately pay your salary, suppliers help you delight those customers. Without them, there would not *be* any customers. So the smartest leaders carefully nurture both customers *and* suppliers in this dynamic, vital, triangular relationship.

Executive Summary

Million-dollar Questions

- What adjectives would describe your experience with your company? What do your customers want or need that isn't being addressed? What could be done better, faster or cheaper?

- Are your customers thrilled?

- What does your response to problems say to your customers?

- Do you really know who your customer is?

- How does the change affect the end customer?

- Are your suppliers friends or foes?

Stop and Reflect

- What message are you delivering to your customers on a daily basis?

- Can you remember the last time you spoke with a customer? If not, you're out of touch.

- Don't underestimate the importance of your internal customers.

- What would make doing business with your company an unforgettable experience?

- Do not try to *guess* what your customer wants.

- How many customer-service and customer-satisfaction agenda items have you reviewed in the last six months?

- Are your suppliers your friends or your enemies?

Wake-up Calls

- Put yourself in your customers' shoes.

- Sometimes it takes a taste of your own medicine to make you change.

- Check your daily agenda for the percentage of time you spend with customers.

- How you handle customer service sends a powerful message about what matters to you.

- Keep your antennae up.

- Eliminate 'us and them' silo thinking.

- Listen to your employees' advice.

- Get into your customers' lives.

- Take every opportunity to make the customer's experience with your product come to life.

- Don't let your company get sidetracked – its business is its business.

- If anyone fails, we all fail.

- Communicate, communicate and communicate with your employees and suppliers.

Leadership Notes

- Make sure you get the picture.

- Treat your customers like royalty.

- Everybody in the organisation has a customer.

- The right products and services, the right place and time, and the right price – these are the keys to customer satisfaction.

- Problem solving is a collaborative exercise.

Are you running your business or is it running you?

THE MONUMENTAL COST OF INEFFECTUAL processes that leaders have allowed to become imbedded in corporate life is staggering. Almost everyone sees that many of these corporate tools – strategy planning and review, annual appraisals and career planning – have become little more than rituals.

What's your role in this modern-day version of Hans Christian Andersen's story 'The Emperor's New Clothes'? For instance, are your days spent racing from one long meeting to the next at the expense of customers and employees? Are you a serial emailer? Do you allow your email inbox to set the focus of your day? Do you allow your mobile phone or Blackberry to interrupt your one-on-one meetings?

If a process or tool isn't working within your organisation, speak up and fix it. Do not suffer in silence and watch everybody go through the motions.

Wake-up Call

Where are you colluding to
waste money and human talent?

A CEO invited me to join the executive board meeting and 'get to know the business'. I found the process more interesting than the fibre-optics the company was selling. Three sets of people made carefully choreographed presentations. All three presentations had these things in common:

- *Fear.* The presenters looked terrified. Nervous fidgets gave them slow starts. What was so nerve-racking about being in front of the board? I wondered.

- *Well-incubated anxiety.* An earlier agenda item ran long, so each team of presenters was left cooling its heels in the corridor until well past the scheduled start time.

- *Incredible polish.* These were annual-report-quality presentations, with beautiful PowerPoint slides and slick-paper documents. Clearly, immense work went into the preparation.

- *'Kick Me' labels.* While the presenters made their cases, the board members took notes on what to attack first. There were no compliments.

When the meeting ended, I caught up with some of the presenters and said, 'I was really impressed by the quality of your presentations. You were extremely well prepared.'

'You had better be ready when you present to the board,' one of them retorted.

'What do you mean?'

'Well, the board is demanding. You can count on days and days of preparation, knowing full well that whatever you do will be torn to pieces.'

'That explains why you looked so nervous at the start.'

'Nervous? It's gruelling up there. But now it's over, and I just want to get back to my regular work.'

The real irony of this exercise was that one of the company's stated values was to prevent waste – yet here was a terrible example of wasted human talent on the highest level.

Later, I chatted with the CEO.

'Terrific presentations at the meeting today,' I said.

'Great stuff,' he agreed.

'I was surprised to learn how much time they put into preparing all that material.'

'Really?'

I told him about my earlier conversation with the presenters.

'You mean they put that many hours into just one presentation for the board?' he asked.

'They do. And you know what they expect to get out of it?' I related how they described having their work 'torn apart'.

'So you're telling me I've got high-income, high-power brains abandoning their regular work for days on end just so they can design beautiful PowerPoint slide shows? And then they get their heads handed to them on plates?'

'I was going to ask you about that.'

Stop and Reflect

Is it time to stop the bleeding?

His response was swift. He drew up a template for all future board presentations, including guidelines for print and electronic material. And he had a conversation with the board members: 'The way we've been criticising these presentations is a terrible waste of talent, and we're not here to waste talent.'

It wasn't long until being selected to present to the board was a sought-after perk.

Look for processes and meetings that no longer deliver what was intended. Just because something has become routine in your organisation, it doesn't mean it is effective. Whoever is leading or running the meeting must review from time to time the effectiveness of the meeting.

Wake-up Call

Slay the sacred cows.

The meeting was a two-hour session at which I had been invited to present the Hudson Highland Centre for High Performance's latest findings on leadership to 50 of a company's Asian leaders. I arrived as scheduled during their break.

There were six white-jacketed and white-gloved waiters serving coffee and biscuits. Seven information technology specialists set up my laptop for my PowerPoint presentation.

I asked one of them, 'Why seven technicians? This isn't a terribly complicated thing we're doing here, is it?'

'No, sir, not at all. We just want to make sure your presentation runs perfectly and you have everything you need.'

I wondered what it cost the company to make 50 executives and me feel like royalty.

What are the sacred cows that are soaking up money in your company? Since I didn't have a coaching relationship in the company, I didn't have the opportunity to challenge the culture that created such waste. I can only guess that, in the past, some accident had occurred that would explain the overkill of tech support. That happens in many organisations. At the time something is first set up, the logic behind it appears sound. But months or years down the road, long after the value has evaporated, nobody speaks up to challenge it.

Wake-up Call

Meetings have become the scourge of business life.

One of the biggest time wasters I see mushrooming mindlessly in business is meetings. Meetings are a bit like a virus. They grow and grow. If you look at most executives' schedules, the vast majority of what they do is attend meetings, which in turn expands to fill every available slot of time.

If you look at the cost of meetings, you get to a big number fast.

Stop and Reflect

Is the value coming out of a meeting justifiable?

When I talk with leaders about meetings, I ask, 'How many people usually attend the meeting and what do they earn?'

If you have a two-hour meeting, think about the cost in salary terms of the attendees. Then think about what results you expect to come out of that meeting. Build into your calculation the fact that, when your senior people are in a meeting, they aren't doing anything else.

Leadership Note: *Count the cost of every meeting.*

Once you fully grasp the cost of a meeting, that knowledge leads to more disciplined meetings, changing agendas or abandoning some meetings altogether.

In most meetings, people aren't fully participating all the time. In poorly run meetings, people are looking at their Blackberries and their mobile phones and drifting off – thinking about the mountain of work awaiting them in their offices.

Stop and Reflect

Have you thought about banning Blackberries (or similar devices) and mobile phones from your meetings?

Another cost of meetings that isn't usually taken into account is starting late or overrunning the allotted time. That's sloppy. There is a cost – both mental and emotional – to those kept waiting. Remember the unfortunate souls who sat waiting, waiting, waiting to give their presentations before the board.

Think objectively about the last meeting you attended. Where were the breakdowns? As a coach and observer, I recall a meeting I recently attended as a typical example: the meeting started 20 minutes late, two agenda items were unclear, three people left the room to take calls on their mobiles and the meeting overran the allotted time by an hour. Common sense would tell you that is not the way to operate, but it is not so easy to see when you're in the middle of the action.

> **Leadership Note:** *Ultimately, you are being disrespectful of others' time by routinely starting meetings late or running over the allotted time. Role doesn't matter. People should not have to wait on you – period.*

At the Alexander Corporation, our antihierarchical, relaxed culture gradually led us into the trap of sloppy habits when it came to meetings. I established a ground rule that our meetings started on the minute, no matter who was in the room. People became embarrassed about turning up late, and the problem was quickly resolved.

Wake-up Call

Make your meetings effective and constructive.

A CEO who was highly effective at running meetings scheduled frequent early-morning sales gatherings and made attendance voluntary. The high-energy meeting was open not only to the sales team but to anyone in the company, because he asserted that 'we're all in sales and have customers.' He published a detailed agenda 30 days in advance, so that participants knew what to expect and were mentally prepared to add to the discussion.

Attendees knew, however, that, if they were one minute late, they were not allowed to join the meeting. The man, who had a military background, also ended the meetings on the dot. His sales team produced 10 times the industry average.

Million-dollar Question

Have you ever seen a meeting agenda that was too short?

Furthermore, you must add in the cost of your agenda. Is it too long? Off the mark? An effective meeting is merely a vehicle for information exchange, idea generation, discussion and decision making.

Stop and Reflect

Challenge yourself to have a one-item agenda on occasions.

If you are too busy to prepare properly for a meeting that you have called, you are too busy. A sloppily run meeting comes with a big price tag. Most of the agendas I see are topic lists that don't convey either what the subject matter will be or the purpose of the discussion.

Does the person who called the meeting expect to reach a conclusion on each item? Or is the meeting for a discussion that will be used as input for a decision-making process? Is it merely informational? Does the leader want to brainstorm ideas?

Leadership note: *A well-led meeting has structure and purpose.*

Every topic ought to have a clearly defined purpose. Also, you should state what, if anything, the participants ought to do in advance for each topic. Give specific instructions such as, 'Come with three ideas', 'Read the document circulated last week' and 'Bring your questions.'

Wake-up Call

Apply discipline and thought to your agenda and revolutionise your meetings.

Another cost that needs to be taken into account is poorly documented meetings. Wonderful topics can be fully discussed, but follow-up will likely be minimal if records of what goes on aren't kept and distributed.

Rate from 0 to 10 your meetings in terms of clarity of purpose, adhering to the time schedule, energy, focus/flow, openness/honesty, and value to the business. Guide your colleagues towards the meeting style that works.

Million-dollar Question

What is the point of this discussion?

Too many meetings are called for the leader's sake. Command-and-control leaders often demand meetings for the sole purpose of having underlings report what they are doing. Before you call a meeting, ask yourself what the value will be for the other attendees. If there is very little payoff for the other people in the meeting, restrain yourself.

How do we get caught up in time-wasting meetings? Here are the danger signals:

- The tyranny of doing rather than reviewing. So much time is spent thinking about the agenda that you don't step back to look at whether the meeting truly adds value.

- In a culture that isn't open, people are reluctant and fearful of being honest regarding how little value the meeting delivers. If you aren't getting feedback, ask specifically regarding a regular meeting, 'What is working and what's not working?' Some leaders never ask because they are afraid of what they'll hear.

Much of this discussion on meetings is all common sense, but all of us get out of touch with common sense from time to time. Especially if we are so busy running from meeting to meeting that we don't build in time to stop and reflect on our work lives.

Stop and Reflect

Eliminate time-wasters.

Wake-up Call

Speak up.

The same CEO who wouldn't allow latecomers to join a meeting in progress if they were even one minute late established some other radical meeting rules. If at any time a participant found the meeting boring or irrelevant, that attendee could leave the meeting with no reprisals and no questions asked. That rule held true even if an outside speaker was presenting. Of course, the CEO informed outside speakers in advance about the company's unusual meeting attendance rule.

To make certain that meetings remained productive on all counts, the CEO declared that anyone who wasn't participating in the discussion could be challenged. The CEO was fair game, too. If the attendees agreed that the person challenged wasn't contributing, that person was thrown out of the meeting.

I noticed something missing in the office of one entrepreneur who used what he called 'lightning meetings' very effectively. There were no chairs. He didn't even have a chair at his desk. He stood at a work table and spent the rest of his time wandering around the company. When I asked him about it, he said, 'I don't want anybody to be too comfortable. No chairs helps people stay on track.'

Leadership Note: *Honesty is the best policy.*

Wake-up Call

Identify meetings you are no longer going to attend and the agenda items you are going to drop from the meetings you run.

One CEO was running himself ragged trying to attend all the meetings that his senior executives called. On top of that, all meeting agendas were sent to his office for approval.

A few questions into our first coaching session, he realised that meetings were getting in the way of his real job. A left-brainer, whose attention to detail and planning had resulted in his promotion to the top spot, he hadn't quite learned to shift into the broader thinking required in his new role. He relinquished his self-imposed duty of overseeing all those different meeting agendas. He also cancelled his attendance at all but a handful of meetings that required high-level strategising.

> **Leadership Note:** *Keep meetings to an absolute minimum. If you must meet, keep the agenda short and to the point.*

If you look at most people's schedules, they are full of meetings. In some cases, that's all that appears in their schedules. One of the most common complaints that I hear from leaders is: 'I don't have enough think time. I deal too much at the operational level and not enough at the strategic level.'

Wake-up Call

Book a meeting with yourself.

One way to begin to create that time is to book an appointment with yourself for think time. Treat that time with as much serious-ness as you would a really important meeting with your most important client. Do not hope that the time to think about next year's strategic plan or other high-level thinking will magically appear. You must put this time into your schedule.

Million-dollar Question

Are you making time for what should be the most important meeting of your week?

Ironically, the really important stuff in a leader's work life regularly gets stuck in the margins. Have you ever told yourself in regard to some important planning, 'I'll do that in the cab going to the plane'? If so, you urgently need to schedule a meeting – with your-self.

Leadership Note: *Don't allow the really important things to be squeezed out by the urgent.*

I ask many leaders where they work at their best, and it's often not at their offices. Athletes set up an environment where they can achieve their best performances, and that includes the training environment.

What work environment would help you get the most out of that two hours you've booked on Friday to work on your strategic plan? You call the shots, so, if working at your home office would give you an undisturbed space, do it.

Stop and Reflect

Put as much thought into planning your time with yourself as you would any other meeting.

Although I admire leaders who maintain an open-door policy, any sort of policy taken to an extreme can have a negative effect on the business. When someone asks for 'just five minutes of your time', recognise that the exchange is likely to take longer. What seems urgent to them probably wouldn't even make it onto your list of important items. Get a clear handle on what's really urgent, or you'll soon feel that you're drowning.

Stop and Reflect

Don't make yourself too available.

Critically important for your organisation are meetings where you have a broad audience – sales and distribution meetings, shareholders meetings, quarterly company meetings and the like. You can accomplish a great deal in those meetings. Many leaders, however, get so caught up in the day-to-day stuff that they delegate planning these events to underlings and don't devote the proper amount of mind time to them that they deserve.

I'm not suggesting you get bogged down with the nitty-gritty details. But I am saying that the most effective leaders carefully orchestrate such events for maximum impact.

Wake-up Call

**Make your big, important meetings
send a big, important message.**

One corporation on an annual basis treated its entire franchise network to a four-day sales conference at a top-notch resort. Every second of the long weekend was considered by the company's top executive team and designed with a grand purpose.

The franchisees went home with the powerful message that they mattered in the organisation and with a clear understanding of where the company was headed in the coming year.

Stop and Reflect

Ironically, some of the biggest missed opportunities when it comes to meetings are with the biggest audiences.

For a company-wide conference about next year's business plan you'd expect droll presentations, endless PowerPoint shows and dark suits.

We helped a company that had developed a reputation for being stiff and formal to design a six-hour conference to disappoint those expectations. Instead, we made the conference fun and gave it a purpose. People would leave this meeting confident about the future and wowed by the possibilities.

Stop and Reflect _____

Who says business as usual shouldn't be fun?

To do that, we ruled out everything that didn't add to the audience's confidence or boost its excitement. And we built in the unexpected – like a musical skit performed by the executive team based on customers' best and worst experiences with the company.

Reports were brief and meaningful. The hotel staff wore company-branded products rather than their regular uniforms. And, as a parting gift, everybody got a T-shirt that said 'No tie required' – symbolic of the CEO's call in the coming year for employees to take off their ties, roll up their sleeves and work as a team.

Million-dollar Question _____

Do we really need trees?

Another way in which we can so soon feel that our business is running us rather than vice versa is when we all start suffering from information overload. Nowhere is that more evident than at the executive level.

We live in the information age. I read recently that the average executive is deluged in any one day with 50 times the information that he or she had 20 years ago. Leaders are forever trying to cope with the volume of information coming into their offices.

Stop and Reflect _____

Demand and read only one-page summaries of all documents for a month and see how often you are caught out.

Whenever I visit CEOs in their offices, I often see *The Economist*, the *Harvard Business Review* or *Business Week* stacked up. Most leaders try to assimilate a mountain of information, fearful that they'll miss something important. The avalanche of information is omnipresent. The question that remains is: how can I discriminate and only focus on what's really important?

Delegate the bulk of your reading material to a junior executive or trusted assistant. Ask that person to scan the materials and highlight the few items that should be called to your attention.

Million-dollar Question

Before you read anything else, ask yourself, What's the worst that will happen if I don't read this?

Try this as an experiment. For the next week, read 10 per cent of what you normally try to assimilate. At the end of the experiment, see if it hurts you in terms of the business.

Although much of our technology has the capability of making our lives more efficient, oceans of ink have been used in writing about how we have instead allowed technology and information to overrun our lives. What promised to make our work lives easier has instead served to make many of us more manic and available almost round the clock.

Indeed, over the past 20 years or so, the much-ballyhooed paperless office has failed to materialise. Much of the information that overflows into our offices results from staff who copy their emails to higher-ups on everything.

Leadership Note: *Practise what you preach. Keep all memos short and don't contribute to information overload.*

Conversely, knowing when to provide information can be vital.

A US-based CEO was fuming about the onslaught of data requests from the acquiring company's central office. He was used to running his own show in an entrepreneurial fashion. The new multinational owners, however, were equally hands-on and information-driven.

'It's unreasonable!'

'What do they want to know?'

'Endless details!'

For a while, he ignored their requests. That won him the label of stubborn and unmanageable. They increased the pressure.

He switched to a tactic of lethargic minimalism: give them a little and take forever to do it. Not surprisingly, that didn't help.

'What do you suppose they think you're doing?' I asked him. 'Have you tried thinking about this from the acquiring company's perspective?'

'They don't have a clue.'

> **Leadership Note:** *If the business is running you rather than vice versa, make your case at the top.*

'Maybe that's the point. Maybe they don't know what you're doing and want to see that your division can perform.'

'Listen. I have people who can't complete their jobs due to these data deadlines.'

I suggested the only alternative I could think of. 'Make your case at the top. Let them know your work flow is interrupted every time you furnish their reports –'

'– and if they want me to succeed,' he said, finishing my thought, 'give me room to manoeuvre. You're right. I'll address this directly.'

His meeting with the executive team at the head office not only reduced the data requests, it changed his label from 'stubborn' to 'driven to succeed'.

Wake-up Call

How are you contributing
to the tyranny of email?

Email is a wonderful tool, but in too many executive offices it rules the day. More than one CEO I know has admitted to spending the first two hours of the day wading through emails. For some, it's become almost a mindless addiction. In fact, in several large corporations executives are getting 200 or more emails a day – much of it as a result of being copied on emails destined for someone else as the primary recipient.

In some corporate cultures, copying others on emails has become necessary to show work, or is seen as being politically astute. Many simply press the 'copy all' button because it's easier than picking and choosing who really needs to get the email.

> **Leadership Note:** *Email is great, but it demands discipline.*

Serial emailers who send out upward of 150 emails a day – 130 of which aren't important – are proliferating in the corporate world. Email is a great communication vehicle when used sensibly, but it strangles your efficiency if you're not disciplined about it.

Before you send or read an email, ask yourself, Is this email really useful? Be ruthless in using the preview line function to weed out the chaff. If you are in a position of authority, you may need to retrain your staff on email etiquette. When you find yourself receiving useless emails, don't delete, but return to the sender with a message that says, 'I don't need this. Please refrain from copying me on this in the future.'

Stop and Reflect _____

Would your work suffer if you read emails just once a day?

Email overload has increasingly become a complaint I'm hearing from executives, and it's now viewed as having the potential to decrease efficiency. I encourage leaders to introduce some personal ground rules about emails. For instance, most emails don't need an instant response. For some leaders, just reading emails once a day is a more effective practice.

One CEO I coached was regularly having his assistant print out all of his emails. Then he would go through them, dictate his response to her, and she would reply. Sheer madness!

Wake-up Call

Eliminate excess email.

After working with one company for two weeks, I was added to its corporate headquarters email list.

Now, whenever there's a fire-alarm test in its headquarters, I get a priority email about it. I am also kept abreast of weather in the cities where the company has major offices.

Stop and Reflect _____

Take a risk. Delete all emails for a week and see if you still have a job.

I don't need to know any of this, and, as I hit DELETE, I wonder who really does.

A lot of people in businesses treat everything as urgent, and all the emails they send have that little exclamation mark that signify them as urgent.

Leadership Note: *Many emails add no value.*

Wake-up Call

**Decide how you're going to
handle the deluge. Announce
your new policy and stick to it.**

Because I travel so much internationally and my whole world is wrapped up in my ability to communicate, I travel at all times with two mobile phones, a Blackberry and my laptop computer. In my line of business, I must be available to my clients. I love the freedom these tools afford me. I also know, however, how and when to switch off and completely relax. Just because I *can* technologically make myself constantly accessible, it doesn't mean I *should*.

The smart use of technology means using it in such a way that it saves you time and allows you to be more focused and more on top of your job. If you are proceeding in a chaotic, stress-laden way, then your technology isn't working for you.

Million-dollar Question

Are you a master of technology or does it rule you?

Many top executives are ineffective in using technology, because what they have almost works for them – but not quite. They go to a hotel and have a hassle getting on the Internet, or they don't quite grasp some new software the IT departments installed on their laptops.

Million-dollar Question

What personal-organisation tools and technologies add to your sense of peace?

A sign of mastery in the world in which we live is personal organisation. There's always some attention on time management. Whatever system works for you is fine. Don't feel pressure to use the latest system favoured by the time-management experts. Again, the purpose of these systems is a way of stilling the mind.

One of my favourite tools is voicemail because I can use it any time, anywhere. However, I recognise that there is power in face-to-face meetings and benefits from personal visits that no phone call can match.

Stop and Reflect

Don't allow any high-tech tool to cause you to lose touch with your business. Nothing substitutes for face-to-face time with employees and customers.

Wake-up Call

View your objectives with crystal clarity.

The 42-year-old CEO was sent in for a three-year stint to grow the manufacturing business and make it ready to sell. This might have made him ruthless, but with a warm smile, a firm handshake, and a touch of humility, he was always strikingly relaxed and ready for a chat.

How did he do it? He had a crystal-clear picture of his objectives and screened out all distractions by asking himself, Is this the best use of me?

He worked from nine to five, never more or less, never weekends – which he devoted to his wife and two kids. He took no paperwork home and kept his desk uncluttered. Especially impressive was that he was physically fit.

He called no-agenda meetings to gather fresh ideas. He scheduled no-meeting Fridays for thinking. 'Everybody needs a blue-sky day,' he declared. All meetings ended within an hour, and reports were kept within a single page.

If he wanted to know more or needed something else, he asked.

He managed people with care. In conversations, he was genuinely present, never diverting his attention elsewhere. He built a brilliant team that delivered exactly what he wanted, and he relied on a personal assistant to watch, listen and report, while filtering out everything that didn't keep him on target.

He asked me to coach him to the 'next level'.

'You don't seem to know how effective you are,' I told him.

'Is there anything I'm missing?'

'Can you teach? Everyone wants to know your secret.' It was the only thing he wasn't doing.

He became a mentor, demonstrating how to integrate an array of leadership techniques around a philosophy of calm clarity. It was the next level in his growth, and, frankly, he was good at it.

I've worked with countless leaders who have slipped into the dangerously easy routine of letting the business run them rather than vice versa. Stop your slide into this common pitfall. A bit of clarity of thought and firmness of purpose will put you back on top, which is where you're meant to be.

Executive Summary

Million-dollar Questions

- Have you ever seen a meeting agenda that was too short?

- Ask yourself, What is the point of this discussion?

- Are you making time for what should be the most important meeting of your week?

- Do we really need trees? You'd think not, judging by the amount of paperwork we generate.

- Before you read anything else, ask yourself, What's the worst that will happen if I don't read this?

- Are you a master of technology or does it rule you?

- What personal-organisation tools and technologies add to your sense of peace?

Stop and Reflect

- Is it time to stop the bleeding of talent?

- Is the value coming out of a meeting sufficient?

- Have you thought about banning Blackberries (or similar devices) and mobile phones from your meetings?

- Challenge yourself to have a one-item agenda on occasions.

- Eliminate time-wasters.

- Put as much thought into planning your time with yourself as you would any other meeting.

- Don't make yourself too available.

- Ironically, some of the biggest missed opportunities when it comes to meetings are with the biggest audiences.

- Who says business as usual shouldn't be fun?

- Demand and read only one-page summaries of all documents for a month and see how often you are caught out.

- Would your work suffer if you read emails just once a day?

- Take a risk. Delete all emails for a week and see if you still have a job.

- Don't allow any high-tech tool to cause you to lose touch with your business. Nothing substitutes for face-to-face time with employees and customers.

Wake-up calls

- Where are you colluding to waste money and human talent?

- Slay the sacred cows.

- Meetings have become the scourge of business life.

- Make your meetings effective and constructive.

- Apply discipline and thought to your agenda and revolutionise your meetings.

- Speak up.

- Identify meetings you are no longer going to attend and the agenda items you are going to drop from the meetings you run.

- Book a meeting with yourself.

- Make your big, important meetings send a big, important message.

- How are you contributing to the tyranny of email?

- The email of the species is deadlier ... Eliminate excess email.

- Decide how you're going to handle the deluge. Announce your new policy and stick to it.

- View your objectives with crystal clarity.

Leadership Notes

- Count the cost of every meeting.

- Ultimately, you are being disrespectful of others' time by routinely starting meetings late or running over the allotted time. Position doesn't matter. People should not have to wait on you – period.

- A well-led meeting has structure and purpose.

- Honesty is the best policy.

- Keep meetings to an absolute minimum. If you must meet, keep the agenda short and to the point.

- Don't allow the really important things to be squeezed out by the urgent.

- Practise what you preach. Keep all memos short and don't contribute to information overload.

- If the business is running you rather than vice versa, make your case at the top.

- Email is great, but it demands discipline.

- Many emails add no value.

So now how will you live your life differently – or is it business as usual?

LEADERSHIP AND EXECUTIVE COACHING HELPS the executive lead with maximum effectiveness and ensure personal enjoyment and satisfaction.

There's not just one style of leader who can be successful. The point of this book is to help you be the best leader you can be. Take stock of where you are now as a leader versus where you were, once you've worked through this book.

Million-dollar Question

> Am I creating an environment where people are in the right mental and emotional state to perform at their peak?

The Hudson Highland Centre for High Performance says only 30 per cent achieve creating an environment where people can operate at their optimal levels; anecdotally, I'd put the number closer to 20 per cent.

Ask yourself, Are the people I lead stressed out? What legacy am I leaving?

There's not just one style of leader who can be successful. Not everybody is cut out to be a super-nova CEO like the legendary Jack Welch who led General Electric from the front. Not everybody can be a charismatic entrepreneur like Richard Branson, known for nurturing his employees and encouraging them to think like entrepreneurs.

Stop and Reflect

Ask yourself, Is what I do creating an environment where people can perform at their best?

When people are stressed out, they perform at a suboptimal level. In sports, flow is actually a state where athletes are focused and not fearful. Apprehension introduces tension into muscles and the mind, whereas flow produces the opposite effect and allows for excellent concentration. Leaders can create environments where people are scared to make mistakes, afraid of the leader's anger and confused.

Wake-up Call

To see ourselves as others see us takes work.

Seeing ourselves through the eyes of others often provides revelations that help us get to where we want to be. Surround yourself with advisers who offer support and who are strong enough to challenge you when you need to be challenged.

At the end of this book, what have you learned? What insights have you had? What have you done differently? On a scale of 1 to 10, how determined are you to continue with the actions and resolve this book has provoked?

Identify someone who you know will tell you the truth about how you are doing as a leader. Every few months, review your progress – ideally with someone who can be objective and hold you accountable for the changes you've agreed to make.

> **Leadership Note:** *Remember, greatness comes from who you are, not what you do.*

These aren't questions you answer just once in your life. I'd recommend you visit them at least once a quarter, and survey the big picture annually. After all, we all live in two dimensions – the outer world, which is in constant flux, and the inner world. Life changes all the time. Your family situation may change. Market conditions are constantly changing. We also change internally. As we journey through life, we see things differently through an accumulation of life experiences.

Million-dollar Question

Where do you need help?

Wake-up Call

Call in reinforcements to shore up your weaknesses.

A man I coached wouldn't have got the job if he hadn't been a superstar, but he was astute enough to realise he could use wise counsel. So he set up a trio of advisers to get him through that first year of what was arguably one of the toughest CEO jobs in the

United States. He picked one adviser to coach him on the cultural aspects of the business, another to give input on strategy, and me to watch over matters of leadership.

It isn't a bad thing to ask for help and guidance. In fact, it's usually the weakest leaders who don't.

> **Leadership Note:** *With many advisers, plans succeed.*

He was there to change the fortunes of the company, recruited for his proven strategic abilities, and the first thing we talked about was his weakness. 'I'm not very good with people,' he said.

We discussed the options. He could learn new skills, ignore the lack of them or recruit someone else to cover for him.

He kept the objective in focus. 'I'm here to get the big job done. Show me how I can raise my people skills while I take care of business.'

We worked up his elevator speech, that succinct self-presentation of his passion and purpose. And he practised his one-on-one and in-meeting interpersonal skills – mainly, how to ask questions and listen well.

Stop and Reflect

Is there a small group of trusted people you can go to for advice?

But he also decided to bring in a deputy chief executive who was brilliant on the people front. With one strategising for success and the other inspiring people to reach for it, they became a formidable partnership and sparked one of the most remarkable turnarounds in US business history.

Remember that hierarchy kills honesty. Identify a small group of trusted advisers/mentors/peers to whom you can go for advice and feedback.

Share with them who you want to be as a leader. What do you want to be remembered for as a leader, or what's your legacy? What is your definition of success? What would you like to be remembered for in terms of your leadership style?

Never make the mistake of thinking, My business is unique. Copying others' success is smart play. Reread this book with an eye for what you can apply to your own situation.

Wake-up call

Learn how to coach your colleagues.

In our coaching workshops, we often teach executives how to coach colleagues and their own people. The same issues occur everywhere:

- how to address a hard-to-work-with boss;

- how to deal with an underperforming team member;

- how to handle the work–life balance that tips off kilter;

- how to innovate within the tyranny of routine; and

- how to create more strategic thinking time.

Teaching something also drives it home for the teacher.

We've devised a way for newly developed coaches within an organisation to gain experience while doing good in the community. We match university students and executives from several businesses together for an intensive four-day programme.

Students bring real-life issues and their vast curiosity about the business world. The executives practice coaching skills and connect with a generation to which they have little access. It's a win–win.

> **Leadership Note:** *There is nothing new under the sun.*

Even though you may not find yourself exactly mirrored in these pages, the best leaders – though they may have differing styles – share some key characteristics, according to the Hudson Highland Centre for High Performance. These leaders who are effective at creating a high-performance culture or ethos are skilled at creating an environment in which people feel valued and one in which they optimise critical, relevant thinking.

These leaders are focused on what's important to the work as a group with very little distraction tolerated. They are skilled at creating an environment in which people are able to seize opportunities and allowed to take risks – an environment in which learning is a core value.

Stop and Reflect

Duplication is good. List five projects your business is engaged in that must have been completed elsewhere. You don't always have to reinvent the wheel. That's part of what I bring to the party.

Wake-up Call

Find someone to talk to today.

A young CEO needed contacts. I suggested lunches with other top executives – informal meet-and-greets – and pitched the gatherings to them as the chance to meet a new, rising star who was creating remarkable changes at his company.

I teased them with the topics we could cover:

- To what do you attribute your success?

- How do you balance strategy and operations?

- How do you manage the financial press and shareholders?

The young CEO got to learn at the feet of some of the brightest in the business world, and they were invigorated by his unique ideas about the open corporate culture he had established as well as by his enthusiasm. I served as facilitator for the meetings and formed several ongoing relationships.

Wake-up Call

Make the big changes.

In coaching, finding good models to imitate can be useful. Here are some of my clients who made the biggest changes. See if you find a kinship in any of the following situations.

- The young millionaire entrepreneur rethought his purpose and subsequently shifted his focus from being purely one of making money to one of social responsibility aimed at creating better education for underserved youth with learning disabilities.

- Conditioned by his family that only a big corporate job counted, the man chucked it all in for a life of his own choosing – running a soft-adventure company with his wife.

- With the business vulnerable and stock shares plummeting, the executives wisely shelved their consensus-building styles and took command. It's what leaders do. They didn't find the style comfortable – 'I need this now!' instead of 'What would help us all reach our objectives?' – but it worked. And when the crisis ended they slipped back into their old leadership roles, wiser.

- The woman saw herself in a bigger role and pictured a seat on the board. I suggested she draft strategy papers for the chief executive and put a voice to her vision for the company. She also volunteered to head up projects outside her domain. It surprised the CEO to discover she'd been overlooked for a long time. With her show of initiative, he had plans for her – including a seat on the board.

- Strategically brilliant, a CEO saw businesses as complex puzzles he could solve in his head. He had risen far this way, always succeeding with smart analysis. Now at the helm of a huge chain of food stores, he recognised his blind spot: people. Unpredictably fickle, they were the one variable that could derail the best-laid schemes or ensure success with their dedication and accountability. He was astute enough to see what he needed. He brought in a COO who was as brilliant with people as he was with strategy.

- A CEO's stern, clear thinking methodically brought order to the company. After three years and a successful transformation, he began to wonder if he could reinvent himself, too. A typical reserved Englishman, he found it came naturally to organise a business into a well-oiled machine. 'But do you suppose I could become a charismatic leader?' he asked. 'A visionary?'

I suggested an acting coach to loosen him up and teach him to express passion. Meanwhile, we could work together on the vision part.

I asked him about how he wanted to be remembered at the company. We talked about his dreams for his children and about his values. He brought to the surface his commitment to honesty, justice, and equality – just the sort of thing a visionary leader needs.

Some time later I saw him take charge of a workshop. Although I knew him well, I had to search for a new description.

He was inspiring.

- The sandwich chain had an unblemished history and a strong plan for growth. But, when the CEO took a hard look at the saturated market, she realised the effort required for continued success was more than she wanted to give. She asked the board. They agreed to sell.

- The CEO of a small company was doing well enough, with a pretty good salary and a pretty good set of challenges. In fact, the son of a coal miner who had grown up desperately poor, he'd gone further than he ever thought he would. But sometimes he wondered just how far he could go.

  'Far, far beyond this,' I said.

  He didn't believe me. Also, he hadn't gone to college or business school. 'How would I stack up against executives in publicly-quoted companies with all their education and experience?'

  I sent him to talk it over with a headhunter. His perception changed. He went to the owners of his company. 'Let's discuss how I can have a share of this business.' Their indecision dragged on, so he put himself on the market and landed a spot as COO in a big company – top salary, stock options, the works.

- Two executives worked 90-hour weeks, barely saw their families and reported feeling out of shape. Yet neither had hope of change, because success depended on self-sacrifice. I challenged each to help the other, and something remarkable happened. Where they didn't see change possible within themselves, they cheered for it in each other. Each committed to reducing weekly hours, and, with the other's insistence, succeeded.

- The man was promoted to lead a team he had once been a part of. He had to learn how to lead his former peers and simultaneously correct inappropriate behaviour and dress. He successfully navigated a potential minefield of professional disasters and worked his way to a position on the board.

- Just before he started, the new CEO of a pharmaceutical company discovered that his native business communication style differed drastically from that of the people he would be leading. His curt, assertive and confrontational manner wouldn't be welcome in transactions in the foreign country in which he'd be operating.

He began to adjust his style before the first meeting with his staff, then in the meeting took an even bigger step. 'I understand we have cultural differences, and, as I adapt to yours, I'd like your help. Please tell me when you find me too forceful or direct. In turn, I'd like to hear from each of you. In a sentence or two, give me your description of your management style. The better I know you, the better I can relate to you.'

That's a bold step for a leader, and a great beginning for any organisation.

I hope you'll use these thumbnail sketches as encouragements about how much you can change. Likewise, use the Executive Summaries at the end of each chapter. Over the years, I've witnessed people undergo miraculous transformation. I would love to hear about how you've used this book to make changes in your own life.

Executive Summary

Million-dollar Questions

- Am I creating an environment where people are in the right mental and emotional state to perform at their peak?

- Where do you need help?

Stop and Reflect

- Ask yourself, Is what I do creating an environment where people can perform at their best?

- Is there a small group of trusted people you can go to for advice?

- There is nothing new in business. Someone has already faced your challenges. Learn from history.

- Duplication is good. List five projects your business is engaged in that must have been completed elsewhere. You don't always have to reinvent the wheel. That's part of what I bring to the party.

Wake-up Calls

- Let us see ourselves as others see us.

- Call in reinforcements to shore up your weaknesses.

- Learn how to coach your colleagues.

- Find someone to talk to today.

- Make the big changes.

Leadership Notes

- Remember, greatness comes from who you are, not what you do.

- With many advisers, plans succeed.

- There is nothing new under the sun.

Appendix A

Core Coaching Beliefs

A number of core beliefs have been borne out of many years working in the coaching and human-performance fields within and outside the corporate world. These underpin all my work:

- Most people most of the time are trying to do their best.

- Everybody has far more potential than he or she is currently exhibiting.

- It is not essential to understand a situation fully to be of enormous value.

- Increased awareness is a powerful enabler.

- The answer to most problems lies within the individual(s).

- Most businesses do far, far too little to acknowledge/thank/congratulate people and celebrate success.

- People leave important parts of themselves at the door of their workplace.

- Most senior teams are not well regarded by staff.

- Most managers are too controlling and delegate insufficiently.

- 'We value our people' and 'We believe in work–life balance' are lies in most organisations.

- The tyranny of 'building shareholder value' will increasingly be seen as a flawed game plan/point of focus.

- People need meaning in their work lives.

- Openness and honesty are keys to high performance.

- Most business cultures are hopeless at giving feedback.

- Most organisations spend a disproportionate amount of time on the underperformers/'problem' people rather than on the high-performers.

- Behaviour is difficult to change and needs to be approached at a number of levels.

- Giving someone the answer is only as good as his or her buy-in and ability to implement.

- A spectacular amount of time and human energy is expended on things that are not important.

- Common sense disappears in the 'heat of the battle'.

- Individuals and organisations have a tendency to overcomplicate issues.

Appendix B

The Two Most Common Questions

I often get asked two questions. The first is: 'Do you practise what you preach?'

I'm happy to be able to answer with a resounding, 'Yes!'

I constantly look for ways to make the sphere in which I operate a better place. For example, in my business, Alexander Corporation, we allow people to give up to 10 per cent of their time to charity or their community.

One of our employees came up with a great idea: our company partnered with schools and sponsored a holiday greeting-card programme. We paid a pound for each card the schoolchildren painted, and they could choose which charity received the money from them. We sent the cards to our clients and suppliers. By the time we finished, we had sent thousands of cards, and our clients loved them. In fact, several of them picked up on the idea.

The second question I get asked is: 'Will these questions and principles work for just anybody?'

Again, I'm happy to say that these key questions can serve as a powerful tool to help anyone transform his or her life. I was also closely involved with a programme for troubled youth. Teenagers identified as unmotivated were challenged with three-week work experience, community-service activities and outdoor-adventure opportunities.

Unmotivated? Hardly. Once they were meaningfully engaged, they proved capable of remarkable achievement.

And what works for troubled teens works for leaders and their people: help them find meaning in their challenges, and achievement follows.

One of my clients emailed me just before Christmas and asked for questions to consider during the holiday period. In Appendix C you'll find some bonus questions.

Appendix C

Questions for Reflection

- What gets you up in the morning?

- Which aspect of your job do you most enjoy? How much of your time do you spend doing that?

- Which aspect of your job do you least enjoy? How much of your time do you spend doing that?

- What keeps you awake at night?

- How do you have fun?

- How much time are you spending 'taking care of you'?

- What would you do if you didn't have to go to work tomorrow?

- Are you enjoying the money you earn?

- How much money is 'enough'?

- Whom/what do you see in the mirror?

- Are you healthy enough?

- If the next year was the best year of your life, what would you achieve? How would you feel? What would be your principal theme? What would be your motto?

- What miracle would you like to occur?

- If I met you in five years' time, what would you like to tell me you were doing? How did you achieve it?

- What did you use to do that you loved and should do again?

Related to the chapters

- What is your purpose in life/in your job? Is it real for you day to day?

- How do you think your colleagues/family see you?

- Are your people inspired by you, your company and its work?

- Are you doing the minimum (but the most important) possible?

- Is your company getting the highest and best use out of you? Are you playing to your strengths/what you love to do?

- What are you not doing that you would deeply regret if this were the last day of your life or your loved one's/colleague's?

- How much quality time are you spending with your loved ones?

- How are you being with your colleagues? Are they getting too much or too little of you? Are you enhancing their performance in every contact?

- Are your customers and clients happy? How do they see you and your company?

- Do you feel on top of things or are you drowning?

- What will you do differently today?

Appendix D

About the Alexander Corporation

The Alexander Corporation is a leading provider of one-to-one executive coaching, leadership, team and culture development. Founded by Graham Alexander in 1986, Alexander has worked with many of the FTSE 100 and Fortune 500 companies.

Extensive client relationships include: Cadbury Schweppes, Kingfisher Group, PricewaterhouseCoopers, Lloyds TSB and BAE Systems.

Mission statement

We maximise performance, development and fulfilment in people and organisations everywhere.

Our vision

To ensure the achievement of measurable results in alignment with explicit business needs beyond what people thought was possible. Thus we have a life-enhancing impact in the world of work.

Our services

- Executive Coaching

- First 100 Days Coaching

- Master Classes

- Keynote Speeches

- Coaching Training

- Coaching Audits

- Leadership Development

- Culture and High Performance Development

- Team Coaching, Development and Facilitation

To learn more about Alexander and the author of *Tales from the Top*, please use the following contact details:

Alexander
200a West End Lane
London NW6 1SG
England

Tel: +44 (0) 20 7435 7194
Website: www.grahamalexander.com and www.talesfromthetop.com

About Graham Alexander

How did someone who was shy, failed his A-level exams, served petrol and drove minicabs develop the world's best-known business- and life-coaching model? How did this person end up working with many of the largest organisations and most success-ful people of our time? Sometimes I still have to pinch myself as a reminder that it's true.

In the late 1960s, I started to take an interest in the emerging field of psychology, predominately from the US west coast, and joined the growing interest in Eastern religion and philosophy. I pursued answers to big questions with a passion, pondering: What is the meaning of life? Does God exist? Who and what am I?

I read widely, participated in workshops, became familiar with Gestalt therapy, psychosynthesis and encounter groups, and explored the teachings of gurus and philosophers throughout history. I spent hours struggling to focus as I meditated or un-tangled myself from a yoga position.

Parallel to this journey, I was experiencing success in my first real job with IBM. After my first year, and at a relatively young age, I became a manager. I was fascinated by the challenge of bringing out the best in my people. At the time, however, that was not a fashionable subject.

After five years at IBM, I took a two-year sabbatical and worked with a charitable organisation, the Trident Trust. The trust provided disadvantaged young people, nearing the end of their schooling, with opportunities outside the classroom. The opportunities included work experience, community service and an adventure experience similar to Outward Bound, which was intended to broaden their horizons and prepare them for life after school.

The combination of my self-exploration through humanistic psychology and Eastern routes – along with my discoveries as a leader and manager and what I learned from working with youngsters – showed me that within all of us lies a great potential, as well as the capacity to interfere with it.

Rather than return to IBM, I decided to continue exploring a wide variety of approaches to human performance and learning. What did great sports coaches do? Did business training add value, and, if so, what? What were the characteristics of world leaders old and new? During this time I set up a charitable trust with a friend and, after taking several deep breaths, jumped off the diving board and started to run self-awareness programmes.

We ran weekend workshops, open to the general public, in a beautiful country house (borrowed rather than owned), where participants explored their lives. We had overworked business-people, single mums trying to make ends meet and students struggling with their parents and education. The stuff of life. Thus with no formal training, I embarked on my vocation – working with people in intimate settings on issues relevant to their work and personal lives.

These workshops proved to be a great success, and I discovered that I had a talent for helping others. I discovered that by creating a safe and nonjudgemental environment, and by making small and often subtle interventions – such as asking a question, or giving some feedback – I made a big difference. I learned that keeping quiet when people were emotional, listening and being there for them, and simply caring, had profound effects.

People asked if I worked on a one-on-one basis, and I started to work with people in confidential settings to see how I could help with their dilemmas or challenges – doing what is now known as life coaching.

At around the same time, I read a book that greatly influenced my coaching career – *The Inner Game of Tennis*. When I first read Timothy Gallwey's seminal book, it was like a homecoming. There in front of me was a text that reflected my own discoveries in terms of what helped people raise their awareness, define goals, remove interference and release potential. Coaching became the driving force in my life.

Witnessing remarkable results in the sports world achieved through 'Inner Game' coaching, and experiencing rapid break-throughs in my own 'life coaching', I turned my attention once again to the business world. In the early eighties, on a quest to intro-duce coaching into the world of work, I became one of the pioneers and influencers in coaching, now omnipresent in business.

In 1986 I set up the Alexander Corporation, which became the market leader in business coaching in Europe. The Alexander Corporation offered a broad range of services, including one-on-one and team coaching, building manager and executive coaching capability and supporting organisations in developing coaching cultures. We focused at the top end of large businesses and linked our work to their strategic agenda and measurable performance outcomes.

Then in 1999, with the consensus of my fellow shareholders, we sold the company to an American consultancy. Since that time, I have built a close-knit team of highly capable associates and have continued my exploration and delivery of coaching in its many forms. Over the years I've coached more than 30,000 leaders in either one-on-one or team situations in more than 200 corporations.

A significant part of my life has been devoted to helping people find the answers to important questions. May you find the answers that will lead you to greatness.

Graham Alexander
London
January 2005

Index

PIATKUS BOOKS

If you have enjoyed this book, you may be interested in other titles published by Piatkus. These include:

Be Your Own Counsellor: A step-by-step guide to understanding yourself better
Sheila Dainow

Body Talk at Work: How to use effective body language to boost your career
Judi James

Business Etiquette for the 21st Century: What to do – and what not to do
Lynne Brennan

Career Comeback: 8 steps to get back on your feet
Bradley G Richardson

The Confidence to Be Yourself: Practical ways to boost your self-esteem
Dr Brian Roet

Confident Conversation
Lillian Glass

Difficult Conversations: How to say difficult things
Anne Dickson

Digital Aboriginal: Radical business strategies for a world without rules
Mikela Tarlow

Engaged Customer, The: The new rules of internet direct marketing
Hans Peter Brondmo

Feeling Safe: How to be strong and positive in a changing world
William Bloom

Fierce Conversations: Achieving success in work and in life, one conversation at a time
Susan Scott

Getting Things Done: How to achieve stress-free productivity
David Allen

Guerrilla Marketing Revolution, The: Precision persuasion of the unconscious mind
Jay Conrad Levinson and Paul R.J. Hanley

I Don't Know What I Want, But I Know It's Not This: A step-by-step guide to finding gratifying work
Julie Jansen

Interviewing Skills for Managers
Tony Pont and Gillian Pont

Life Coaching
Eileen Mulligan

Life Coaching for Work
Eileen Mulligan

Make it Happen!: A step-by-step guide: from creativity to innovation
Kathryn M. Redway

Napoleon Hill's Keys to Success
Napoleon Hill

Network Your Way to Success: Discover the secrets of the world's top connectors
John Timperley

NLP Coach, The: A comprehensive guide to personal well-being and professional success
Ian McDermott and Wendy Jago

Perfect CV, The: Today's ultimate job search tool
Tom Jackson

Positive Living: The complete guide to positive thinking and personal success
Vera Peiffer

Putting First What Matters Most: Proven strategies for success in work and in life
Jane Cleland

Ready for Anything: 52 Productivity principles for work and life
David Allen